**From reviews of Mary's biography of
William Joyce, "Lord Haw", Germany Calling.**

"This book is a classic. Mary Kenny's book made me laugh aloud, and weep, and think. It is sympathetic, in all the right ways, to the monster it portrays."

A.N. Wilson, London Evening Standard.

"Mary Kenny has written an absorbingly elegant study. To all Joyce's shabby dreams, loyalties and cruelties, Kenny brings both compassion and a clear mind. A biography whose even-handed beauty of expression combines Irish gravity with Irish spark."

Hywel Williams, The Guardian.

"Comprehensive and authoritative, Germany Calling nonetheless manages to be as compelling in its sweeping mastery of material as a thriller. ....A triumph...Sensitive and entertaining."

Terry Prone, The Irish Independent.

"Germany Calling presents a wealth of new material...a fascinating, vital account of Joyce's nasty, short and brutish life."

The Jewish Chronicle.

Reactions to Allegiance (a play about Michael Collins' meetings with Winston Churchill in 1921-22).

"Kenny suggests that even those on opposite sides of the negotiating table can discover common ground if they reognise the humanity in each other."

Lyn Gardner, The Guardian.

"A discussion as plausible as it is absorbing...The wishfulnesss of the play doesn't turn into sentimentality."

Benedict Nightingale, The Times.

"An interesting and touching work...a warm portrait of the two men. Mary Kenny has written an intriguing vignette."

Quentin Letts, The Daily Mail.

"A keenly imagined script...an absorbing entertainment."

Lynne Walker, The [London] Independent.

AUTHOR'S NOTE

It has been suggested to me on a few occasions that I should produce an autobiography; but I believe a memoir should be funny, honest, have an exceptional story to tell, or add significantly to the wisdom of our experience, and I have not yet arrived at such a point where I feel I could contribute to any of those four categories.

This play, nonetheless, does draw on elements of autobiography and of transmitted memory, as well as on reading and research I have done on Ireland's neutrality during the Second World War (formally described as "The Emergency" in what was then called Eire, now the Republic of Ireland). The radio announcements at the start of Scene 10, for example, are based on British monitoring of Radio Eireann in 1940 and archived at the Imperial War Museum. For researchers interested in the period, I thought it might be useful to add a selection of my published writings and reviews about that "Emergency" time, and these follow the playtext.

Perhaps the personal element of autobiography is the hardest to confront, and I do very much subscribe to Emily Dickinson's words:

Tell all the Truth but tell it slant –
Success in Circuit lies
Too bright for our infirm Delight
The Truth's superb surprise

As Lightning to the Children eased
With explanations kind
The Truth must dazzle gradually
Or every man be blind.

*   *   *   *

I would like to thank Peter Marinker for directing a reading of A State of Emergency on October 17, 2009 in London. It was done with such thoughtfulness, polish and professionalism and it enlightened, for me, all sorts of elements within this text. It was a privilege to watch Virginia Byron, Colette Kelly, Patricia Leventon and Madeleine Potter perform the roles, and I was much moved by their enthusiasm for the work. I was delighted when Clare Murphy subsequently joined the ensemble, and so gratified that she liked and enjoyed working on the play – and a public performance is planned for 2010. I also thank Teresa Marinker for her kind support and intelligence.

In addition, I would like to thank Lynne Parker, of Rough Magic in Dublin, for reading the script and being warmly encouraging: she very kindly said it read beautifully and "offers a valuable insight into an under-investigated time and social class", although she did feel it was more suited to film or radio than the theatre. This may be so, but I have always been stage-struck, and stage-struck is how I shall remain: every time a drama enters my imagination, I see it in a theatre.

My gratitude also to my friend Tony Duff, who read and commented on the text: his knowledge, experience and judgement of the theatre are superb and I always trust what he says. That he enjoyed the playtext, found that it was "very alive – the characters and the period" means, for me, that it is a worthwhile endeavour - and I have followed most of his suggestions.

All works have flaws, as has this one. (It has been suggested that Scene 4 could be dropped altogether, and I regard that as an optional choice in any future production.) Indeed, there may be further re-writing of this text – as the great Michael Frayn has remarked, a play is never really finished, but always changes in the course of development. But it is as truthful as I can make it – and it does have one virtue: many women in the theatre lament that there are not enough parts written for women, and particularly for older women. A State of Emergency certainly has parts for women, and the female actors who have done a reading of it have demonstrated that with distinction.

On a brief point of speech: for non-Gaelic speakers I have transliterated a few Gaelic phrases, and also explained a point of vernacular speech.

Mary Kenny
Deal and Dublin
2009-2010
www.mary-kenny.com

"*Going to Dublin was changing worlds – a dance of lights in the Liffey, bacon and eggs and Guinness, laughter in the slums and salons, gossip sufficient to the day. Dublin was hardly worried by the war; her old preoccupations were still her preoccupations. The intelligentsia continued their parties, their mutual malice was as effervescent as ever. There was still a pot of flowers in front of Matt Talbot's shrine.*"

From Louis MacNeice's memoir of the Second World War years in Dublin in *The Strings are False.*

A State of Emergency

CHARACTERS

JULIA FITZGERALD	aged 42/43, and subsequently aged 86
GEMMA FITZGERALD	her daughter, early forties
	Gemma and Julia (when young) may be played by the same person: other doubling is feasible.
DYMPNA FITZGERALD	her daughter as a child aged about 10. (May be played by an adult presenting as a child.)
HANNA O'SULLIVAN	a woman in her later sixties, a family relation (whom the child Dympna addresses as "Aunt")
PAMELA HART-CALLAGHAN	a contemporary of Julia.
DEIRDRE	a receptionist: a young woman.
MRS BRADY	care home owner – in her fifties
ROSIE BYRNE	aged 19, a waitress, and subsequently in her early sixties working as a care home assistant.
RADIO ANNOUNCER	(female): heard only.
THE TIME:	1940 and 1984.
THE PLACE:	Dublin, Ireland

OUTLINE OF SCENES

An interval is suggested after Scene 8.

SCENE I

Easy-listening music of a generalised kind at first. We are in the lobby of a small Dublin hotel, The Argyll - a converted Victorian house in south Dublin. There may be distant sounds which indicate the sea - perhaps some seagull cries. We are in 1984.

Gemma Fitzgerald, enters the lobby with a suitcase. She is attractive and dresses in a medley of warm autumnal colours. Her voice, though Irish, is marked by certain inflections of someone who has lived abroad. Her body language is weary, although she is generally confident by temperament. The receptionist, Deirdre, takes an offhand manner as Gemma approaches..

GEMMA: Hello, I ----

DEIRDRE: Just a sec, please.
A pause. Deirdre answers the telephone, businesslike, robotish...

DEIRDRE: The Argyll Hotel - Deirdre speaking.... How may I help you? No.... Mr and Mrs Cunningham aren't here at the moment ...they're abroad..... Oh, in about three weeks.....

A little more business conversation ensues, and Gemma looks around the lobby examining its features with some distaste. Deirdre finishes the phone conversation:

DEIRDRE: Yes, I'll tell them you were in touch – but you could always call back next month. *(To Gemma.)* Now: what can I do for you?

GEMMA: You know: this is a fascinating subject for enquiry. Why does the ringing of a telephone always have a greater priority than the person standing in front of you? Something to do with the urgency of a ringing sound, perhaps? Or does it mean that by 1984, machines carry more significance than people?

Deirdre looks at her a little sullenly.

DEIRDRE: Do you ---

GEMMA: Yes. I have a reservation for three nights. The name is Fitzgerald.

DEIRDRE: *(Unfriendly.)* Yes... yes, we've got that. Ms Geraldine Fitzgerald.

GEMMA: It's Gemma, actually. Miss Gemma Fitzgerald.

DEIRDRE: It says Geraldine here.

GEMMA: The Norman invasion. Association of ideas.

DEIRDRE: Hah?

GEMMA: "Geraldine FitzGerald." The Fitzgeralds were Geraldines... after the Norman invasion of Ireland. 1169. I feel sure they still teach the Norman invasion of Ireland.

Deirdre thinks Gemma is an eccentric.

DEIRDRE: Would you like to sign the register, Ms Fitzgerald? And how will you be settling the bill? Cheque or credit card?

GEMMA: Ah, the good old *Céad Míle Fáilte. Airgead! Airgead!* [Money.Ir.]

DEIRDRE: It's just the usual procedure...

GEMMA: Credit card --- probably....*(She does some signing, sighing)*.So Des and Eileen are in Florida, are they?

DEIRDRE: Yes, Mr and Mrs Cunningham are away. How did you know it was Florida?

GEMMA: They always went to Florida. Even before it was unfashionable.

DEIRDRE: So you know Mr and Mrs Cunningham?

GEMMA: Intimately. Though whether they'd know us, now, is a different matter. How many hotels does he have these days? Five? Eight? Twelve?

DEIRDRE: I couldn't say. You'll be in room 29, Ms Fitzgerald. That's in the "Monticello Annexe". Here is your key...

GEMMA: Room 29? Twenty-nine rooms in this Victorian conversion?

DEIRDRE: With the annexe, there'd be 36. Mr Cunningham plans to build a new wing, at the back, next year. We're just obtaining planning permission.

GEMMA: Well, well, well. Enterprise Ireland. No better man!

DEIRDRE: Well, I hope we can do everything to facilitate your stay in Dublin.. *(Consulting her register.)* Is it business or pleasure?

GEMMA: It's "A la recherche du temps perdus..."

DEIRDRE: Mmm...*(She ticks a box anyway, though exasperated.)* Our porter, Jack, can bring up your suitcase. There is a lift at the back of the lobby.

GEMMA: No, I'll take the stairs. I always liked the staircase.

DEIRDRE: Breakfast is from 8 a.m. until 10pm. Check-out by mid-day..

GEMMA: Yes, at least, the old banisters still remain ….At least there's that.

DEIRDRE: Oh, by the way, I forgot to ask you…. *(consulting a form on the register)*. How did you hear about this hotel?

Gemma looks distinctly pained.

The generalised "muzack" swells. The tape now begins to play a yearning, orchestrated version of the wartime song "Lilli Marlene", as Gemma makes for her room. She reaches the bedroom, which seems like a tiny box carved out of the remains of a once fine Victorian bedroom.

GEMMA: The old window! And the scratched graffiti is still there on the window-pane!   And the willow tree in the garden! Daddy's lovely old willow tree!

Quite suddenly, the brittle, ironic façade crumbles and she breaks down into violent tears. She cries for a few moments uncontrollaby.
More music, now properly in the style of 1940.

Fade. Ends Scene I.

SCENE 2

It is 1940. We are in the breakfast room of the same house. A profusion of birdsong, with some seabirds. A little girl of nine or ten years of age, Dympna, is playing with her dolls' house, while an elderly woman, Cousin Hanna, is looking after her. Hanna is a retired schoolteacher and speaks with a certain degree of precision, and with a pleasing rural Irish accent.

DYMPNA: When will Mamma be home, Aunt Hanna?

HANNA: Don't you know your mother. Once she's in town shopping she's lost to the world! Shop, shop, shop.

DYMPNA: She always brings me home a present, though.

HANNA: And then she might go off to afternoon tea with one of her cronies. Or worse.

DYMPNA: What's worse?

HANNA: "Cocktails." They get that from the pictures that come out of Hollywood. The devil's own invention.

DYMPNA: Did the Devil invent "cocktails"?

HANNA: He might well have done, but it's the pictures that can be such an occasion of...worldliness and materialism.

Dympna is a thoughtful little girl and ponders this for a moment.

DYMPNA: I like the pictures. We had Charlie Chaplain at Edna Reilly's birthday party. Billy Reilly has a photo of a film star in his bedroom, and her name is Rita. Her bosom is all stickey-out. Is she called after Saint Rita?

HANNA: I doubt it!

DYMPNA: Naish has different pictures in his bedroom.
(She is concentrating on re-arranging the furniture in her dolls' house and pauses between phrases.)
He has a photo of a man with a big Alsatian dog. Naish says the man is called Hile Hitler. It's a nice picture too. Though it's not as nice as the Rita lady.

I wish we had a dog. We'll ask Mamma if we can get a dog.

HANNA: *(Indulgently.)* Don't be minding everything your brother says. Tis all cloud cuckoo land...
What would you want a dog for? Sure dogs are only required on farms.

DYMPNA: Mrs Hart-Callaghan has a dog.

HANNA: Yappy little creature. A rat on a rope. Mrs Hart-Callaghan is English, anyway.

DYMPNA: Do English people have more dogs than Irish people?.....
But Hile Hitler isn't English, is he? And he has a dog. 'Cos if he was English, Naish wouldn't like him so much, would he?

Hanna laughs.

HANNA: In Ireland we have <u>working</u> dogs, *a stoir*.. Dogs that work on farms, earning their living. *(Ever the schoolteacher.)* We're an agricultural country, you see, Dympna. That's why we never got along with the English. Because they don't understand a nation based on agriculture. They're an industrialised country, and their standards are different. Quite different.

DYMPNA: Well, in my dolls' house, I'm going to have a pet dog. It's time for all the little babies to go to bed now. See, Aunty Hanna, I'm putting them all to bed.

HANNA: How is it, Dympnaleen, that you would ask Mamma for a dog, but you wouldn't ask Dada?

DYMPNA: Sure Dada is too old to be bothered with worries. *(The child is repeating what she has heard, and then adds her own thoughts.)* Dada is nice, but he's *very* old.

HANNA: How do you know your dada is old?

DYMPNA: 'Cos Dada took me to Bewleys last week, the waitress lady said to me: "Now aren't you the lucky little girl, and isn't <u>your grandfather</u> very kind to bring you out for a big ice cream sundae like that?"

HANNA: *(Rummaging in her sewing basket.)* People should never make assumptions about the nature of family relations.

DYMPNA: Aunty Hanna?

HANNA: Yes, *a stoir*?

DYMPNA: *(anxiously)* If Dada is very old, does that mean he'll die soon?

HANNA: Yerrah, not at all. Don't people live to a great age nowadays? We're not in Queen Victoria's reign any more. *(She says this with a kind of wonder.)* Look at me! Amn't I'm as old as the hills? And I intend to go on living as long as the good Lord will spare me.

(A distant sound of the Horst Wessel song is heard from upstairs.)

DYMPNA: That's one of Naish's tunes. On the gramophone for Hile Hitler. Hile Hitler's dog is called Blondi.

HANNA: How do you know that?

DYMPNA: 'Cos Naish writes to Hile Hitler and Hile Hitler writes back, and he sent a photograph and he said the dog was called Blondi. Billy Reilly knows about Blondi too. If I had a dog, I'd call her Shirley.

HANNA: Ignatius is making it all up, Dympna! Tis all eyewash! And that auld Hitler is a bad man and an auld blackguard. He puts priests in jail and he does away with poor crippled children! There's a lot of evil men in the world nowadays, and we must pray for them, and for all the godless atheism that has them the way they are....
(Hanna switches with a deliberate change of mood.)

Now, would you like to do some painting and drawing, or would you prefer to practice your reading?

DYMPNA: I don't mind. Mamma told Mrs Hart-Callaghan that you're very good at teaching me reading. *(Anxious to please her mother.)* Mamma sounded very proud of me!

HANNA: Didn't I teach little girls like yourself for over forty years? Tis a pleasure to me to do it.

Here's something in the newspaper now, that would be nice for you to read...

It's about a little Italian girl not a lot older than yourself.

(Dympna goes over to Hanna and takes the paper from her. Dympna then stands as she has been taught to do in elocution lessons, formally, reading aloud with clear diction and a child's guilelessness.)

DYMPNA: "Pope Pius ...ex, one, one..."

HANNA: "Pope Pius the Twelfth...." *(Hanna is turning half her attention to some needlework.)*

DYMPNA: "Pope Pius the Twelfth today received Blessed Gemma Galgiani into the Communion of Saints. Blessed Gemma was born the daughter a small SHEM-IST near Lucca, Italy, in 1868.

HANNA: "Chemist." That's a medical hall.

DYMPNA: "From her childhood, Blessed Gemma showed singular devotion to the Sacred Passion. At 18, she suffered a series of severe illnesses. Later she was favoured with the Stigmata of the Passion.

HANNA: That's beautiful, Dympna. Go on.

DYMPNA: "On her hands and feet appeared the wounds of the nails, on her brow and head the marks of the Thorns and on her whole body the wounds of the Scourge." *(She pauses for a moment as though to digest this.)* "She died on Holy Saturday, 1903, and was Beatified by Pope Pius ex one..."

HANNA: Pope Pius the Eleventh. God rest him.

DYMPNA: "... the Eleventh, in 1933, only 30 years after her death. Many who knew her were at the ceremonies, including her only surviving sister, Angelina, the priest who baptised her, and at least one of her teachers.....

(Dympna, continuing seamlessly.)

"Many racegoers at the Kildare Hunt Ball, which was held at the Gresham Hotel, Dublin, last night, a fitting finale *(prounouncing it "finally...")* ....

HANNA: <u>Finale</u> – that's from an Italian word, too, so you pronounce the "e" at the end....

DYMPNA: ".....<u>finale</u>, to Punchestown. The attendance included: Sir Francis Brooke, Sir George and Lady Mahon, the First Secretary of the Italian Legation and Mar----- Mar-chesa Mal-espina, and the new Press Attach at the German Legation, Herr Dieter von Hauptmann."

HANNA: Attach-ay, Dympna. *(Interested in this society snippet in spite of herself.)* Who else was there?

DYMPNA: "Also present were Count and Countess Taaffe," *(she pronounces it "Taffy")* –

HANNA: "Taaffe" – a distinguished Kildare family, with Austrian connections...

DYMPNA: Miss Phillida MacGi---MacGill-icuddy, Dr and Mrs Lavelle, and Mrs Timothy Hart-Callaghan." That's Mama's friend. There's a picture of her.

HANNA: Let me have a squint. *(She examines newspaper.)* Would you look at the mink stole on her! Every penny of that man's money goes on her back! If not on "cocktails".

DYMPNA: What's an attach-ay?

HANNA: That's a French word, and the "e" on the end has a mark on it, called an accent, which means that you should pronounce it "ay". Attaché. It is somebody who is formally attached to an office, usually a diplomat. You know what a diplomat is, don't you, Dympna?

DYMPNA: Is it like a spy?

HANNA: It's somebody who represents his country in another country. You read that very well, Dympna. Very well indeed. You're a good girl. *Maith an cailín, tu.* [Ir: "You're a good girl". Pronouncing guide: *Mah on collyeen thu.*]
I'm going to give you a shilling for that. *(She takes a shilling coin from a pocket in her knickers, which are voluminous and bloomer-like.)*

DYMPNA: Thank you Aunty Hanna. But it wouldn't be fair to take your pension money...

HANNA: Yerra, what else have I to spend it on...And you deserve it for working hard at your reading.

DYMPNA: It says here there is a big war on, and it might come to Ireland. But it's only a funny war at the moment.

HANNA: Don't worry, it won't harm Ireland. Sure haven't we got Mr De Valera to protect us? Mr De Valera would never let a big war come to Ireland!

DYMPNA: But didn't Mr De Valera start the big civil war in Ireland? That's what Edna Reilly's mother says. She says he was jealous of Michael Collins so he started the big civil war.

HANNA: *(She lays down her sewing for a moment.)* Dympna. Remember how we learned about the Irish nuns who were tortured to death by the Chinese for their faith?

17

DYMPNA: They were tortured and tortured and tortured by very cruel Chinese pagans to give up their faith, but they never did, they died with the Hail Mary on their lips.

HANNA: Well, that's to show us that we must always stand up for our principles. A principle is something that you believe – that you know to be right. And Mr de Valera has always stood up for his principles, and he would never betray them. And now he's going to keep us protected from any big wars going on out there *(she waves a hand to indicate a faraway continent)*, far, far away.

(Dympna ponders this for a moment or two.)

DYMPNA: Are we safe, then, are we?

HANNA: *(Confidently).* Of course we are. *(The strains of the Horst Wessel song again heard.)* Of course we are! It's not a war for us at all; it's just an "emergency". That's what we call it – "The Emergency". That's what Mr De Valera calls it.

DYMPNA: And is Mamma safe?

HANNA: As safe as houses! *(She is about to make a sardonic crack about the cocktail habit, but seeing the child's anxiety, thinks better of it.)* Would you like some milk and biscuits? Come on, and we'll go and see Kathleen in the kitchen.

Dympna is looking at the dolls' house protectively.

DYMPNA: Gemma is a nice name. If I had a baby girl I'd call her Gemma.

HANNA: *(Gathering up her glasses, sewing, etc.)* Yerra, there's more to life than having babies. Now, when you grow

up, men will talk a lot of codology to you about......
getting married and the like. *(She cannot quite bring
herself to say "sex".)* But many a woman has had a
better life without marriage or children.

DYMPNA: It hurts to have a baby, doesn't it? That's what Edna
Reilly says. Her mammy had a lot of babies.

HANNA: If you were a nun, you could go on the Missions and
see India. Or Africa. You could baptise the black
babies, and then you could call all the little girls
Gemma. You'd have a battalion of babies then. And it
wouldn't hurt at all, at all...

Dympna thinks about this.

DYMPNA: *(After a pause.)* Does Mr De Valera talk codology?

HANNA: *(Half shocked, half amused.)* Oh Dympna! Mr De
Valera is our protector!

They go...

Ends Scene 2.

SCENE 3

Early May, 1940: a corner of a bar- restaurant in the Royal Hibernian Hotel, Dublin. A sort of brasserie where the tables are somehow rather feminine – rose damask tablecloths – but there is a bar section, with high seats, just out of vision. Music from the 1930s at low volume.

Pamela Hart-Callaghan is sitting at a table, waiting to meet Julia Fitzgerald, and repairing her make-up with the aid of a powder compact. She is expensively dressed, hatted and suited, with dark, possibly dyed, hair. She is English – married to an Irishman with influential political connections. She has a brittle way of speaking, and a slight impairment in pronouncing her "r"s. She is slim and attractive, with good legs which she likes to display.

Presently, a waitress, Rosie Byrne, appears. Rosie is a young woman in her twenties: a working-class Dubliner with an air of being wise beyond her years, with the confidence of the eldest in a large family.

ROSIE: It's yourself, Mrs Hart-Callaghan. All on your owney-own? No boyfriends today?

PAMELA: Rosie. You minx. I'm waiting for Mrs Fitzgerald. She's always late. Always!

ROSIE: *(Busy about the table.)* Ah well, when God made time, he made plenty of it.

PAMELA: I hope we're not going to lose you, Rosie?

ROSIE: Lose me? Like you'd be on your bended knees to
            St Anthony... "Please find Rosie Byrne – sixpence
            in the poor box." *(Looking askance at Pamela.)*
            Thrupence...?

PAMELA: So many of you Dublin people are going over to
            Liverpool now to work in the munitions factories....My
            maid has left me to do war work in England, and I'm
            quite distraught. *(Not looking in the least perturbed.)*

ROSIE: Ah, well, now, Mrs Hart-Callaghan, you can see the
            point...
            There's looking after yourself and his Lordship: or
            there's making exciting big bombs over beyond in
            Liverpool – and getting paid real good money for it...
            I'm telling, you, now...it's encitin'.

PAMELA: Oh, money isn't everything.

ROSIE: You don't say!

PAMELA: And it's so dangerous, in England these days...

ROSIE: Sure, isn't it dangerous everywhere? My Da says, now,
            when Hitler starts his carry-on, you might as well be
            there as here. Matter a damn where you are when the
            bombs start fallin'....

PAMELA: I can see that you'll be off any day now. What will your
            poor family think?

ROSIE: They'd be delighted to get rid of me. Isn't there eleven
            of us!

PAMELA: Really? Eleven...!

ROSIE: Well, only eleven belonging to us. When the woman
            next door died, God rest her, havin' a babby, Ma and

Da took in her children too. So that's five extra. But sure we don't mind. As long as we all get work, we don't mind a bit. There's always work in Ringsend, with the bottle factory and the gas works an' all. Will I bring you your tea while you're waiting?

PAMELA: What a cheerful spirit you have, Rosie dear. Yes, I might as well have some tea. Do you still have some provisions of China tea?

ROSIE: *(cannily)* Some can be had.

PAMELA: You know I rather like the delicacy of it. And... scones.....? Damson jam? Perhaps we'll indulge ourselves in a meringue or two. Sixteen children. Dear, dear!

ROSIE: But sure, aren't you English, yourself, Mrs Hart-Callaghan...

PAMELA: English to the bone! But meringues are French. *Meringue...*

ROSIE: No, I mean, shouldn't you be up for England and supportin' the Dubliners going over to the munitions?

PAMELA: I'll tell you a secret, Rosie: I don't give a farthing for their silly little war, which could have been quite easily avoided if they'd listened to sensible people like Lord Londonderry. *(Conspiratorially.)* It's all got up by the Jews, you know.

ROSIE: Is that a fact? *(Rosie exits, eyes just perceptibly rolling.)*

PAMELA: Ah, *voilà!* Here she is!

Julie arrives, a little breathless, carrying shopping

parcels, bearing the names Switzer's, Arnott' s and Rachel of Wicklow Street. She is a pretty woman in her early forties, in a soft, beguiling and sometimes skittish way. She dresses in colourful clothes, and a fetching hat with a feather, just bordering on the outlandish. She has a light Cork inflexion in her voice. She and Pamela have a habit of talking in a quick, bantering way to one another.

JULIA: I'll be late for my own funeral! Sorry...

PAMELA: Oh, I've been having a charming time discussing the war situation with Rosie.

JULIA: It's my artistic temperament.

PAMELA: No, it's because you're a slave to your family. Abandon them.

JULIA: Sure, the creatures think they're abandoned already. My daughter wrote in a school essay - "Mamma's hobby is shopping in town." I was mortified.

PAMELA: You know, Julia, this modern idea of mothers dancing attention on their children is bunkum. The Edwardians never saw their children. Intelligent women have better things to do than play at being nursemaids!

Anyway, you've got Cousin Hanna, haven't you? She was a schoolmarm all her life – let her look after them. She's an old maid anyway – she should be grateful.

Julia makes a mildly mocking face, as if to say "typical Pamela!"

JULIA: Hanna is so grateful already....The spring weather is so lovely out there. The flowers are all out in Stephens' Green....Dublin is perfection.

PAMELA: Yes, the "Emergency" seems to have done wonders for the weather. Tea, and then a cocktail? Yes.

JULIA: Anything! Anything is a treat here! Maybe an éclair?

PAMELA: If they have one. All this damned rationing.

JULIA: Is it going to get worse? Is that what Tim says? How's Tim anyway? Thought he looked so handsome at that art opening last week – so manly in his uniform! And so kind about the car....

PAMELA: Oh, you and I can use the Bentley anytime. He's exempt from the rationing.

JULIA: No coal, no white flour, shortage of tea...that's what they say is on the way...

PAMELA: All because of their damned silly war. Poland – who cares?

JULIA: *(Looking at the menu)*. Poor Poland. Cousin Hanna is saying a novena. A Catholic country, after all...Though I don't mind about the coal, so much - turf fires are lovely! The warmth....the aroma... it reminds of long ago, when I was growing up in Castlemara...Do thank Tim about the car...are you sure it's all right?

PAMELA: It's fixed, darling. Don't worry about it. We can motor wherever we like. And why shouldn't we have our fun?

Rosie is bringing along the tea-things

ROSIE: Hello, Mrs Fitzgerald. I love your hat. It's only gorgeous!

PAMELA: Yes, isn't it divine? Nine guineas in Switzers...

ROSIE: Oh, that's shocking!

JULIA: Don't believe a word she says! Seventeen and sixpence in Clery's... I swear! And Rosie – if you have an éclair...?

ROSIE: Seventeen and sixpence... *(She still thinks that quite pricey.)* Gorgeous just the same. You look just like Joan Fontaine. There youse are, now, ladies. I'm not sure about the éclairs, but we're all right for meringues....

PAMELA: And Rosie? *(Beckons for her to come closer, which she does.)* Find out if those two gentlemen at the bar are spies! Ask Betty – she knows everything that goes on...

ROSIE: Say no more! *(Exits).*

JULIA: *(Tucking in.)* Pamela, you're awful! Making me out to be so extravagant...

PAMELA: Well, you have spent nine guineas on a hat..

JULIA: Yes, but you mustn't say it in front of a poor girl like Rosie. You know she's working to support her family in Ringsend – they're poor people. Now, shall I be mother? *(Pouring tea.)*

PAMELA: If we didn't spend nine guineas on pretty millinery, there wouldn't be any employment at all for poor people. Shopping is practically a patriotic duty. Yes, yes, do, but remember – tea in first, not milk in first!

JULIA: *(Holding tea cup up to the light.)* Only if it's real bone china! Yes, it seems to be...

PAMELA: Not only is Rosie working to support her family – there are sixteen of them! Sixteen! It's obscene. And five of them are the cast-offs from a next-door neighbour who died in childbirth...

JULIA: The poor are so kind to one another. Much kinder than the rich. You wouldn't find them taking in each other's children in Aylesbury Road.

PAMELA: You wouldn't find people in Aylesbury Road having sixteen children. Or even six!

JULIA: Sure people can't help having large families – you know what the Italians say...

PAMELA: Do you know, these scones are perfection. They must have an awfully good source to the black market. I believe there are nuns who pray to St Joseph to help them get a good bargain on the black market...

JULIA: "The marriage bed is the poor man's opera." That's what the Italians say. Mmm, yes.

PAMELA: Yes, well the poor should be forcibly sterilised. That's what they do in Sweden.

JULIA: *(Julia is used to Pamela's deliberately outrageous views and makes light of this.)* Yes, well, it's what they do to bullocks as well! You know, I don't believe those fellows over there are spies. They don't look exciting enough. I'd say they are commercial travellers in..... ladies lingerie...from the North of Ireland. They have that look. Wesley and Sammy from Sandy Row.

PAMELA: Spies deliberately try to look boring. Tim had several of them picked up last Monday. Now, how's everything else? I haven't seen you since ...Tuesday...

Momentary fade to semi-darkness, as we see Julia and Pamela chatting in silhouette, indicating a short passage of time, perhaps with music. Then, lights up again....

JULIA: Dempsey's such a character – he's a scream. He was

telling me that he used to be a jockey in England last time he came to collect me. It's so sad they closed down all the racing for the duration of the war...

PAMELA: Poppy Forbes – she knows <u>everything</u> there is to know in this department and she says – "Always go to bed with jockeys, never with boxers!"

Shrieks of risque laughter as Rosie returns with hot water, etc.

ROSIE: Now ladies....and the answer is "No". They're commercial travellers from Belfast...

JULIA: Told you!

PAMELA: *(Snooty).* Sammy and Wesley in ladies' lingerie.

ROSIE: Is there anything else I can get youse, ladies?

JULIA: Thank you Rosie. You're always so attentive to us. I want to give you a little something..... *(Takes a two-shilling piece from her bag.)* Buy something nice for yourself.. Make sure to spend it on yourself, now...

Rosie is touched, but quick to pocket the coin.

ROSIE: You're very good, Mrs Fitzgerald. You've a heart of gold...

PAMELA: We'll have our customary little drink in a moment...I think it's coming up to the cocktail hour, isn't it? *(She consults a pretty bracelet watch.)*

ROSIE: Well, you've got your usual choice....*(Recites as though a litany.)* White Lady. Black Velvet. Sidecar. Between the Sheets. Bellini. Negroni. Martini. Pink Gin – otherwise known as Mother's Ruin...

JULIA: I think I'll have a Sidecar. Matt and I drank Sidecars on our honeymoon. At Maxim's in Paris..Matt had a dozen oysters and not a sign of an R in the month...

PAMELA: That's an indelible memory for you, Julia dear...

JULIA: *(dreamy)* From West Cork to Paris – wasn't I swept off my feet. Oh, I hope we can go back one day...

PAMELA: You must have a Champagne Cocktail...Champagne is so much better for the complexion than brandy. The only drink which improves a woman's looks. Are we all right for stocks of champagne cocktail, Rosie?

ROSIE: Yeah...five and sixpence a glass, though....

PAMELA: Oh, we're only young-ish once. Let's have two.

JULIA: She's the boss. *(Rosie nods and goes off.)* So who else was there?

PAMELA: Masses of people. We had such fun. I wish you'd come along.

JULIA: I wanted to, all right. But Matt's sister wasn't very well...

PAMELA: There you are, you see – a slave to your family, again! I'm sure that Gertie O'Brien is having an affair.

JULIA: What makes you think that?

PAMELA: Look at her skin. Having an affair is very good for your skin. It gives you 'that schoolgirl complexion'.

JULIA: It doesn't say that in the Pond's adverts.

PAMELA: It's all in the writings of Marie Stopes.

JULIA: Does your husband know that you read banned books?

PAMELA: He's the beneficiary of my progressive ideas! Marie
            Stopes says that even *mingling* with men is good for
            female rejuvenation? Something to do with --- ferry-
            something or other. Men emit certain hormones and
            their aura is good for women...Sort of jazzes up your
            system. It's all in their armpits.

JULIA: They do that with horses. It's the smell of the stallions
            that makes the fillies....you know... sort of...responsive.
            And who is Gertie O'Brien having this affair with?

PAMELA: That writer fellow. You know – he's always at the art
            openings and Jammet's. Good-looking. Communist.

JULIA: Oh him, yes. How do you know?

PAMELA: Tim's office knows who all the Communists are.

JULIA: Is she in love? And what about her husband? What if
            she...conceives a child?

PAMELA: She's having fun, whether she's in love or not. Her
            husband won't find out, and even if he does....I'm told
            he's not very interested in the bedroom department.
            As for conceiving – my dear, she's 45 if she's a day, so
            I should think that's very unlikely. Now, what did you
            buy? *(Indicating the packages.)*

            Rosie reappears with drinks.

ROSIE: Ladies, your order. There you are. Enjoy yourselves.
            (Half singing.) "It's later than you think."

JULIA: *(Lifting her glass).* No, Rosie. The best is yet to be.

PAMELA: And life begins at forty! Not, of course, that we admit to forty! But - chin-chin!

They drink. Music. Brief fade of lights. Lights return very soon afterwards. Pamela is peeking into the shopping bag marked "Rachel of Wicklow Street".

PAMELA: Electric green!

JULIA: No. Lime green! Apple green! You know there was a country superstition that green was unlucky? That's why I love it. It's so fresh.

PAMELA: Arresting, certainly. Expensive?

JULIA: Madame Wine is very good to me. She gives me easy terms.

PAMELA: That's because she <u>wants the business</u>. *(She says "wants the business" in a mock-Jewish accent.)* But I won't tell Matt. You'll look splendid, my dear Julia.

This is bliss. *(Referring to the champagne. She opens a cigarette box and offers Julia a cigarette. They both light up, Pamela using a holder.)*

JULIA: How about the auction – did you get to that?

PAMELA: Edith was arranging a bridge party, so I just couldn't make it. Edith's acquired a new sable fur..

JULIA: Sable! Like a star of the grand opera!

PAMELA: She looks more like an ageing chorus girl. But it's a heavenly coat...And you know, she smuggled it past the customs in a most unusual way....

Rosie is back again, with a slightly more concerned face.

ROSIE: 'Scuse me ladies, but I just thought I'd tell you that I'm going off duty now, as it's the end of my shift... *(Brief pause to deliver her news.)* Somebody has just heard it on the wireless that the Germans are gone into Belgium and Holland.

Pamela and Julia look astonished....

ROSIE: *(Continuing.)* That's what it said. "According to reports, the Low Countries have fallen "...It sounds kind of funny, but it's not funny really. Me Ma will be upset, because, wasn't her own Da killed out in Belgium in the Great War..

And.... it seems like it's getting nearer....doesn't it?

PAMELA: We certainly don't want that!

A brief pause.

JULIA: Oh, reassure your mother that we're safe in Ireland, Rosie. We really are. My husband knows a lot about the political situation. And no one can touch us. We're neutral.

ROSIE: I suppose we should be praying for the poor people that's being invaded, and counting our blessings that we're not in their shoes.... ...yet!

They all think for a moment.

Well, – see youse next week, please God.... And thanks, Mrs Fitzgerald. You still look like Joan Fontaine!

She goes. A brief silence follows.

PAMELA: Well, that's a bore. I do hope the party at the German

Legation won't be cancelled! There are limits to this "Emergency"!

Darkness. Music. Ends Scene Three.

SCENE 4

*We return to 1984, perhaps indicated by music –
possibly Abba. Gemma is driving a car and replaying
in her head, as it were, a conversation she has had with
Mrs Brady, who runs a care home for the elderly in
south Dublin. Mrs Brady is a former nurse, and her
voice, though kind, carries that certain matron-like
authority.*

*Gemma is now wearing a dress and jacket in a bright
apple green, accompanied by a silk scarf in purple.*

MRS
BRADY'S
VOICE: It'll be grand to see you again, Gemma…Your mother
              was delighted with your card from San Francisco. She
              sang a little snatch "California, here I come!" An uncle
              of yours used to sing it, it seems. Your uncle Paddy, is
              that it?

Gemma will nod in recognition at this.

MRS
BRADY'S
VOICE: Your mother is ….doing well enough, all things
              considered…She has disimproved a little bit since
              you last saw her – Dr Clarke says it could be a pre-
              Alzheimer condition. A form of vascular deterioration.
              But having said that, she's really amazing, and keeps
              us all entertained. She can get a bit confused, and then,
              she can come out with some of the most sharp-witted
              observations! Sometimes you'd think – she's all there
              the same Julia!

Gemma smiles and changes gear in the car.
We see the curve of Dublin bay, and hear the seabirds.

MRS
BRADY: *(Continuing.)* But you know, that's the way it goes. In
           her moments of lucidity, more lucid than you or I.
           How long is it since she saw you? It's only a couple of
           months, isn't it?

GEMMA'S
VOICE: Three...more, three and a half....

MRS
BRADY: She'll have forgotten that. She might be uncertain who
           you are at first.... Then she'll settle down. We think
           the world of her here, you know. She has such a warm
           personality. And oh, doesn't she love the style!

           Gemma pulls up and stops the car. Pauses a while
           and lights a cigarette, looking out at the sea.
           Contemplative.

MRS
BRADY: *(continuing)* : Of course, she keeps wanting to go back
           to 'Monticello'. But what can we do? Sure, it's not there
           any more.

GEMMA'S
VOICE: As it happens, I decided to stay in the hotel that took it
           over. Just to see what it was like.

MRS
BRADY: Oh, I believe you wouldn't recognise the place. She
           wouldn't know it at all now.

GEMMA'S
VOICE: They've landscaped the garden that used to be such a
           wilderness. Everything is very tidy and organised.

34

(More to herself: her thoughts.) Bourgeois order has replaced Bohemian romanticism.

MRS
BRADY: There you are. Progress. The world goes on, and leaves some of us behind....Still, we have a very nice care assistant here, now... She's very fond of your mother - dresses her up in her violets and lavenders, so she looks like a Duchess.

Gemma sighs heavily, thinks, blows her nose, and re-touches her make-up...

MRS
BRADY: We've been doing a bit of Memory Therapy with some of our ladies. Asking them about their childhood and that. They seem to like remembering their childhood and early life best. We concentrate on the happy times.

So I'll be seeing you shortly. There will be a couple of little extras on the bill to settle...

Mrs Brady's voice fades. Gemma starts up the car again, sighing as she goes...

Fade. Ends Scene Four. Music

SCENE 5

1984. Gemma arrives at the care home where her mother is now a resident and rings the bell.... a moment later, she is being shown into a bed-sitting-room where her mother sits at by a window, looking out....Julia is dressed in a pretty combination of lavender, violet and purple.

Mrs Brady, an ex-nurse with an efficient manner, enters.

MRS
BRADY: Let's open these curtains a bit now, and we'll let a bit more sunshine into the room. *(Raising her voice a little.)* Julia! You have a visitor today!

JULIA: Have I now? Is it Mother? Get Paddy to go to Kingsbridge station to meet her in the Vauxhall. The Dublin traffic always confuses her. *(Confidingly.)* She still thinks that Dun Laoghaire is called Kingstown! She'll be waiting for a bus for "Kingstown"!

MRS
BRADY: No, Julia, it's not your mother. It's your daughter!

JULIA: *(Playing for time: artfully trying to establish the facts.)* My daughter? Is it Dympna?

MRS
BRADY: Don't you know Dympna is in Africa looking after the black babies! Your youngest daughter, Gemma.

GEMMA: Hello, Mamma! *(Hugs her warmly.)* You're looking lovely! Gorgeous altogether!

JULIA: Ah, well, darling.....You're looking grand yourself....
your rig-out is very stylish. Though ....green... The
old people would never wear it, in times gone by. They
thought twas unlucky.
And your hair....you know, that was exactly my colour!

GEMMA: Well, didn't I inherit it from you, Mamma....!

JULIA: *(still not sure)*. Of course you did, darling-love....

MRS
BRADY: Would you like a cup of tea, Julia, dear? Or maybe an
orange juice or a Ribena?

JULIA: *(Self-consciously mischievous, winking at Gemma.)*
Divil a bit of Ribena! Haven't you a champagne
cocktail? Champagne is the only drink that doesn't
harm a woman's looks...

MRS
BRADY: We're right out of champagne cocktails today, Julia. We
might be able to find a glass of sherry, a little later. Just
a little, mind, so that it doesn't upset your medication.
Will you have a cup of tea, Gemma?

GEMMA: Yes...yes.... Thank you.

MRS
BRADY: Fine. *(She folds her hands together, her fingers
interlocking, like a benign Reverend Mother.)* Well. I'll
be back shortly. *(She goes.)*

JULIA: *(speaking intimately)*. Now that you're here, do you
know, I think we'll go home. I'd like you to take
me home. It's quite a nice place here, but to tell you
the truth, I've had enough of it. Let's go back to
Monticello.

Gemma sits by her mother and takes her hand. Julia begins to cry.

JULIA: Oh, please, darling-love....please, get Ignatius to bring me home now. I want to see Naish and the little girls. The little girls! I want to hold the little girls in my arms!

A pause: emotionally charged. She is confused

GEMMA: But I'm your little girl, Mamma! I'm all grown up now! Don't you remember, Mamma, when you came to stay with me in Rome? Do you remember that?

Julia doesn't speak for a moment, and then recovers herself.

JULIA: We went to Paris on our honeymoon, your father and I. He had a dozen oysters in Maxim's. And you know what? It was August! Oysters in August! "Matt," I said, "it's dangerous to eat oysters in August!" Your father was a wonderful man. He died with such dignity. Welcome be the will of God. Are you married, darling-love? Did you ever marry?

GEMMA: I am, Mamma....yes. Sure didn't you meet Carl many times? And Jonathan...

JULIA: I'm not sure. Maybe I didn't like him.

GEMMA: You didn't dislike him. But he was married before, and you thought that was a bad sign....

JULIA: Isn't he a Protestant?

GEMMA: Yes, he's a Lutheran....

JULIA: Sure, Protestants can do what they like.

38

It's no business of ours!
Now Pamela Hart-Callaghan – she was married three times in all. But her husbands always died. Wasn't that convenient? No disputes about the money.

Are you happily married, *a stoir*?

GEMMA: Sometimes! But he's a good man. He's kind to our son.

JULIA: *(As though half-remembering.)* There's something wrong with your son...

GEMMA: Yes, he has a mild mental handicap. But he's made great strides. You used to look after him with such devotion when he was a baby....

JULIA: You should have had more children, darling-love. Though the way it is, you never think that at the time. Never think that at the time, at all.

At the time, you only see the problems. It's only later you see clearly....

GEMMA: Sure, I might have another baby yet! You never know!

JULIA: Somebody said: "Life has to be lived forward, but can only be understood backwards." Was it Byron?

GEMMA: No – that was a Dane. Kirkegaard.

JULIA: Sure, you're terribly clever altogether. Always were. Your father would have been so proud. You know he ordered a dozen oysters on our honeymoon in Paris? And the month was August! No sign of an "R" at all!

GEMMA: *(indulging her mother of the repetition)* And no harm done...

JULIA: (*Who has been thinking about the words "mental handicap"*). "God's holy fools" – that's what they used to call them. There was a word in Irish. "*Daoine....*" [*This is prounounced 'dinna"]...something. Mother would have known. She was a true scholar. That's where you got your brains from....But darling – would you ever do me a special favour? Big favour?

GEMMA: Of course, Mammy – if I can.

JULIA: Put some more rouge on your cheeks. A woman looks waxy without rouge. (*Fumbling in handbag.*) Here – I have some money for you. Yes, yes, I insist. Sure what have I to use it on?
           (*She fishes out a ten-pence piece – then finds another.*)

           There's four shillings! Go on – you must take it! Take it darling!

           Gemma is touched and upset.

GEMMA: You always wanted to give away everything Mammy darling. And you gave away everything too.

           Rosie Byrne appears at the door, once again carrying a tray of tea: she is now a spry woman in her sixties, kind and practical.

ROSIE: Julia? It's Rosie here with your tea....and you must be the famous baby Gemma! Well, well, well. (*Takes a long look at her.*)

           Well, you're the spitting image of your mother, Gemma. The spitting image! Isn't she, Julia? Ah, but you'll never be as good-looking! Your Ma was a great beauty. Sure didn't I know your mother forty years ago – would you credit that?

GEMMA: Isn't that lovely – but sure Dublin is always small world!

JULIA: There were 16 children in Rosie's family. And how many grandchildren have you got now?

ROSIE: It would be nine, and another expected after Christmas!

JULIA: Children are a great investment. The old people used to say that.

          Rosie goes over and gives Julia a hug, which she warmly reciprocates, almost clinging.

ROSIE: Do you remember the time when you used to come into the Hibernian, and myself working there?

JULIA: The happy times! The happy times of my youth!

ROSIE: *(to Gemma).* That was before you were born. I had a waitressing job at the Hibernian – very lucky to have it. Yes, they were happy times, Julia, weren't they? In spite of the war and everything. Yourself and Mrs Hart-Callaghan were regulars. She was a gas character. "Money isn't everything!" she'd tell me. And herself rolling in it!

JULIA: Do I remember? Could I forget? *(Pause.)* I could forget. I could forget anything.

GEMMA: *(assisting with the tea things).* I hardly remember Pam Hart-Callaghan. Aunty Meg used to call her a "wicked woman".

JULIA: She could be wicked. But so outrageous.... She'd say things nobody else would say. And you'll put up with a lot of wickedness if someone makes you laugh. Your

41

father.....your father....*(She loses the thread.)*

Silence for a moment. Gemma pours a tea.

ROSIE: That's right, Gemma, help yourself. I'll see to your Mammy. I believe you're living over beyond in Germany now?

GEMMA: It's Strasbourg. France, really.

ROSIE: France, Germany – sure tis all the one, now, isn't it?

Gemma smiles ruefully at this...

JULIA: Quite a few people were pro-German during the war, of course. The German Ambassador was charming. Couldn't have been nicer. They gave the best parties in Dublin. You should go to plenty of parties, Dympna. Lots and lots of parties. I was a demon for them. Enjoy yourself while you can.

ROSIE: Concentrate, Julia! This is Gemma, Julia, not Dympna. Dympna is in Africa, teaching the black babies.

JULIA: She was always one for the black babies. She had a black doll she was very fond of. I wonder what happened to it? *(Sad.)* I wonder what happened to everything?

ROSIE: Sure, isn't it lovely to have Gemma here, now, and she so brainy with the languages. Mrs Brady tells me you speak four languages...

GEMMA: More or less. And the *cúpla focal*. *[Coopla fockle.Ir = "a few words".]*

JULIA: Matt spoke seven languages. Latin first. Then *(counting on her fingers)*, French, Spanish, Italian, a bit of Arabic.

42

He studied in the Lebanon, you know. A beautiful country. So civilised. So French...

ROSIE: Well, now... That's where Gemma gets it from, so.

JULIA: Take every opportunity you can, darling. For little by little, they all fade away. Every opportunity fades and dies...You don't like it, but you accept it.

ROSIE: She's full of wisdom, is our Julia.

JULIA: Wisdom, how are you! Tell us - how many grandchildren have you now, Rosie? *(She is examining a biscuit before eating it.)*

GEMMA: I was talking to Mrs Brady about her memory therapy - I might bring along a tape-recorder and record some of Mammy's memories.

ROSIE: Yeah, they were doing that memory therapy business with Mrs Pearson upstairs. Helps to stimulate the old brain cells. Mrs Pearson remembered everything from before the First World War as clear as a bell. But later on, nothing. Funny, isn't it? Amn't I after telling you about the grandchildren, Julia?

JULIA: Sure, Rosie, you've only been here a little while, isn't that a fact? You'll soon learn we're all bats.

ROSIE: You're not bats, Julia. At all, at all.

JULIA: Your uncle T.P. used to say that you should drink eight glasses of water a day, for the sake of your health. Imagine that. Eight glasses of water a day. They got that from the spas. On the Continent. Oh, for the blue skies of the Mediterranean. Weren't you living there once, darling?

GEMMA: Didn't you come to visit us there, Mammy... You had a great time in Rome. And then later we drove up along the Mediterreanean coast...

JULIA: Bordighera. Diana Marino. T.P. loved those places... Himself and Meg took Dympna there for her 21st birthday. They had no children, so they were good to Dympna. I had three brothers – all childless. Delia nicknamed their wives "the Three Barrennesses".

I always wanted Dympna to marry a rich man. But no – it wasn't to be. She was a like a little mother to baby Gemma. Yes, Gemma. Do you remember your First Communion, darling? She was like a little mother to you, the way she dressed you up, so beautifully. We didn't have enough money for a nice Communion frock, but didn't she get the dressmaker to produce one for half nothing. And Naish came home from school specially for the occasion. Maytime.

ROSIE: I'll be getting on, Julia, but I'll pop back in to see you shortly....All right? Now call me, Gemma, if anything's needed....

GEMMA: Thank you Rosie.....

Rosie goes.

JULIA: The salt of the earth, the Dublin people. The salt of the earth. They took in each other's children, poor as they were. Do you get a chance to meet any nice men on your travels, loveen?

GEMMA: Oh I do, Mammy. A lot of nice men! And a few terrible ones too..

JULIA: Terrible men can be terribly exciting. Mixing with men is very good for women. It's something about their armpits....What age am I now? What year is it at all?

GEMMA: You're 86, Mammy... A great achievement! And what year were you born?

JULIA: *(Conspiratorial.)* 1900. But I always used to fib and say 1902! Isn't that shocking! We even used to interfere with our passports...

GEMMA: That was very bold, Mammy - especially since you were actually born in 1898.

JULIA: 1898! That must have been in the old Queen's time! Old Queen Victoria! And what year is it now, so?

GEMMA: As you're 86, it's 1984...

JULIA: Nineteen eighty-four! That's the future! We're in the future now! Imagine that...

Gemma sits holding her mother's hand.

JULIA: Amazing. Just amazing. You know, sometimes I wonder what country I'm in.... If I look out the window and see a green letter box, I know I'm in Ireland.

GEMMA: As good a test as any..

JULIA: Is the old willow tree still there in the front garden?

GEMMA: Oh, yes, Mammy, it is, just as it always was.

JULIA: Your father loved that willow tree. He loved the weeping willow.

GEMMA: And do you remember the little scratched graffiti on the window-pane in the top front room? You said it was there for over a hundred years? Well, it's still there, if you know how to look for it....kind of sideways.

JULIA: Just imagine. Isn't life wonderful? The surprises. But get Ignatius to trim the garden, won't you? The ferns grow so wild along the borders, just in front of the breakfast-room there....And darling – promise me one other thing, will you?

Gemma nods.

JULIA: Don't ever let Tommy Cunningham buy Monticello! He'd turn it into an awful modern hotel, and take away all the lovely old features. He'd rip out all the exquisite old marble fireplaces.. Turn the rooms into rabbit-hutches. I saw what he did with Miss Phelan's house when he converted that. Rabbit-hutches for rooms. All the stucco work *(her hand arcs up as though pointing to a ceiling)* ....

Gemma looks miserable, not knowing whether to admit or conceal. And surprised, too, at her mother's sudden emphatic lucidity.

JULIA: Your father loved the marble fireplaces. We bought that house in 1928, and it was the first thing he remarked upon. And the lovely ceilings with their rose stucco work. I can see it all now, as it was the very day we moved in.

GEMMA: Sure we all have wonderful memories of our home, Mamma.

JULIA: We had such parties there. Musical evenings too. Delia would play the piano and sing from Moore's Melodies. Of course during the war.....*(she loses the thread for a moment).*

46

GEMMA: Oh, I know. You had all the diplomats in the house during the war – didn't we call it "The Emergency" then?

JULIA: Oh yes, all the diplomats. There was one evening when we had the German Ambassador, the British Ambassador, the Japanese ambassador *(she enumerates them on arthritic fingers)* and the American Ambassador – all together, at a cocktail party, in our drawing room!

Outside Ireland, they were all at war, but in our house, in Monticello, they were all quite ….quite happy together…. Of course *(with a naughty look)* I made sure the cocktails were good and strong! Good and strong! *(Laughs.)* Archbishop McQuaid said to me: "You see, Mrs Fitzgerald: that's what your charm and neutral Ireland can do: bring nations at war together." I didn't say to him – "No, Dr McQuaid – it's the good gin that Tim Hart-Callaghan is able to get for us on the black market!" *(Laughs again, enjoying the memory.)*

He wasn't as bad as he was painted, Dr McQuad. He could be very kind. Stern. Cavanman. They're like that. It's the soil. You have to wrench a living out of the poor land. But always kind to people down on their luck. After the war, people shunned the German Ambassador's wife. But he called on her. An act of Christian charity.

GEMMA: You always see the good side of people, Mamma.

JULIA: *(dreamily).* I can see the willow tree still, just as it was, right outside the drawing-room.

Then we went to a dance, and my dance-card was full. What dances we had! What dances!

Music. Darkness. Ends Scene 5.

47

SCENE 6

*1940. Dympna is playing with her dolls, but now alone.
There are several bigger dolls, including a large rag doll
and a black baby doll. She has them arranged in a social
circle and she is conversing with them.*

*In the distance, we hear the low drone of a passenger
aircraft, first growing louder, and then fading away.*

DYMPNA: *(explaining to dolls).* They're the German planes flying
up to the North of Ireland. They fly all over Munster,
see ---ooohhh – *(she demonstrates with her hand)* ---
and then up through Leinster until they get to Belfast…
.'cos Belfast belongs to the King of England, which it
shouldn't be…

And then they fly back again and sometimes they put
the bombs they have left over into the sea, 'cos that
makes it easier for them to fly home again to Germany.
But they don't bomb us, 'cos we're not in the war.
We're only in The Emergency, and Mr De Valera is
protecting us from the big bad world outside Ireland.

And now, Shirley *(to the rag doll)* --- you're my new
little best dollie, 'cos Mamma brought you home to me
as a lovely new present when she was delayed in town
one day…. And now you're part of the family. And
Betsy isn't to be jealous, 'cos you're the new baby, and
new babies are nice.

DYMPNA: (Continuing.) Anyway, Betsy is my special black baby
who we've baptised from being a heathen….now.
*Propping them up, as she makes-believe to give them
tea.*

And we're not to be worried about The Emergency, 'cos Naish says the fighting will all be over soon. Then Hile Hitler will come to Ireland. *(She puts her index finger to her mouth.)* But ssh. It's a big secret. He'll land in Derry and then he'll give the North of Ireland back to us, and it won't belong to the King of England any more.

Pausing. Then getting to her feet, almost as she did before she did the formal newspaper reading with Cousin Hanna...

And this is the way we're to salute when Naish and Billy Riley come to inspect us.

She stands to attention and puts her arm forward in the Hitler salute – carried out quite guilelessly.

Hile Hitler! See!

There's another one too, they do for Hile Hitler's friend.

She performs a Soviet salute, elbow crooked and fist clenched.

Hile Stalin!

Cept we have to keep this secret until The Emergency is over. We'll know for certain when Billy and Naish get a special letter. It will be left under the big stone by the willow tree in the garden....But we're not to breathe a word to anyone!

I hope Hile Hitler brings Blondi the dog with him when he comes to Ireland.

Now!

She hunkers down with her dolls again.

DYMPNA: (continuing) After we've had our tea, we'll then have our <u>cocktails!</u>

She smiles at the dolls fondly. Fade scene. Music.

SCENE 7

Summer 1940. The kitchen at Monticello. Clocks shows 2 o'clock: it is two in the morning. But barely dark. Birds still sing.

Pamela enters the kitchen, in party clothes, slightly the worse for wear. She looks around for a drink, and finds a bottle of some sort, which she examines dubiously: it seems to be some kind of brandy. She pours herself a helping and looks around for a mixer...she finally lights upon a bottle of red lemonade, and pours some in.

PAMELA: Tra-la-la. I've invented a new cocktail. What shall I call it?

She takes out a cigarette, begins fitting it in her holder, and then abandons the effort, and sticks it in her mouth, like a gangster's moll.

PAMELA: Obvious. "The Emergency." The fashionable new cocktail, my dears. One part ... is it cooking brandy? No, rather rough Spanish stuff. And one part red lemonade.
Chin-chin! *(She knocks it back.)*

Cousin Hanna suddenly appears, in her nightie and dressing-gown.

HANNA: It's yourself, Madame Hart-Callaghan. I thought 'twas a burglar...

PAMELA: Oh, Cousin Hanna! *(Sarcastic.)* Why, how fetching you look in your boudoir attire!

HANNA: I was getting worried about Julia and Matt....in these dangerous times...

PAMELA: Oh, *(mock-Irish)* divil a bit of danger...

HANNA: We are in wartime, Mrs Hart-Callaghan.

PAMELA: Oh, Cousin Hanna, how can you be so unpatriotic? And you such a loyal adherent of Mr De Valera. It's an *emergency!* But not much of an emergency! We've been out gallivanting all evening...

HANNA: And where's Julia? What have you done with Mrs Fitzgerald?

PAMELA: Oh --- I think she's outside talking to the chauffeur, Dempsey. You know how s-s-s-sentimental Julia is about the working class and their various troubles.... But don't worry - the husbands are upstairs in the drawing room smoking their cigars. And we're all quite, quite safe! *(She is very sarcastic and quite inebriated.)*

           Hanna makes a disapproving sound.

HANNA: I don't know if you're aware of the seriousness of the situation.

PAMELA: Ah – it's desperate, but not serious...

HANNA: Mrs Hart-Callaghan – consider the news from France...

           A pause. Pamela tries to focus a little.

PAMELA: Oh, ghastly, ghastly, ghastly....but let's not think about it. *(Shrugs her shoulders.)* Nothing we can do about it. *(Drinks vigorously.)*

HANNA: Catholic France! Fallen! Tis a terrible thing.

PAMELA: Look, Hanna! There's nothing we can do about it! Why should one fret over something that...over which we've no control? Why not drown our troubles! Why not forget about misery? Tomorrow we may all be dead!

HANNA: Then I'd suggest we all prepare ourselves for the next world. Prepare our immortal souls for eternity. Not be gallivanting around at decadent parties.

PAMELA: Oh, I shall roast away merrily in Hell. As Dorothy Parker once said.....*(she goes into a slight riff, but can't remember the line of verse)*...'Something something something/girls who live too well/shall roast away in hell ...'

HANNA: Tis your own affair, itself, where you end up, but what about Julia's immortal soul? You're a bad influence on Julia, Mrs Hart-Callaghan, I don't mind telling you..

PAMELA: Got it! 'While those whose love is thin and wise/Shall view John Knox in Paradise!' Julia and I are forty years of age....

HANNA: And more, if I can count ---

PAMELA: And we're grown-up enough not to be lectured like naughty schoolgirls. We are in the prime of life! We are in a neutral country with three parties a night to choose from, and we are exempt from petrol rationing *(she is tango-ing around the kitchen)* because my husband is a very important man... *(Grandstanding)*.

HANNA: You're in a Catholic country, Mrs Hart-Callaghan...

PAMELA: Oh, tosh – I don't give a damn for the Pope in Rome!
            Or Hitler or Mussolini either! They're all just silly men
            strutting around like ...cocks!

HANNA: You have a Christian responsibility to conduct yourself
            with dignity and decorum; and not to be leading
            married women astray...

PAMELA: Oh, tosh and tosh again! Julia is perfectly well able to
            make up her own mind about whatever she chooses to
            do ----- and we're entitled to enjoy ourselves sometimes!
            Especially when there's a war on! All this bloody Irish
            Puritanism -----

HANNA: Mrs Hart-Callaghan! Your language!

PAMELA: *(careless and inebriated)* ---- And Julia's slaved and
            skivvied for her family for fifteen....eighteen....years
            – she provides breakfast, dinner and tea – tends to
            her elderly husband - fills this Victorian mausoleum
            with her needy relations....she's a beautiful woman
            who should be having fun! *(Singing, sort of.)* "Enjoy
            yourself – it's later than you think... Enjoy yourself....
            while you're still in the pink..."

HANNA: *(Shaking her head, in shock and disapproval.)* Mrs
            Hart-Callaghan! I can hardly believe you are the wife
            of our chief of police ...You're not even a lady! To use
            such language!

PAMELA: "Ladies!" - "ladies!" Bunkum and claptrap concocted
            to blackmail women into being little doormats....

            *Hanna is shaking her head in despair and
            incomprehension.*

HANNA: And to be the worse for drink. In your position.

PAMELA: Tosh: tosh: tosh: tosh and tosh. You won't intimidate
          me with your ghastly Irish Puritanism....!

HANNA: More's the pity, Mrs Hart-Callaghan. *(She leans
          closer to Pamela and thumps the table for emphasis.)*
          More's the pity! That's why we had to get rid of the
          British ruling class in this country. Immoral! That's
          what they were! Decadent and immoral! That's what
          Countess Markievicz herself always said – English
          ideas– selfishness and divorce! *(Wagging her finger.)*
          English morals were rotten to the core!

PAMELA: *(Very sarcastic – knocking back more brandy and
          lemonade.)* Oh, well, my dear, when Germany takes
          over the entire British Isles...you may begin to wish
          you'd stuck with the devil you know!

HANNA: *(pulling herself up straight.)* It ill behoves you to make
          such a suggestion. May God protect us from all harm
          and from those godless barbarians...
          *(Holds up her hand firmly to brook any further
          discourse.)*

          I've said my say, Mrs Hart-Callaghan, and I do not
          wish to continue this conversation any further... I am
          just a paying guest in this house, but I am a first cousin
          of Julia's mother, God rest her soul, a most pure-
          minded and holy woman: a member of Sinn Fein in its
          glory days of 'Ireland Sober is Ireland Free!'

          I feel a special responsibility for this family, and
          especially for Dympna; and I don't want ---- I
          would not like to see --- I do not like to see frivolous
          influences prevail....at a terrible time for Christian
          civilisation....

PAMELA: Oh, for Christ's sake! –

HANNA: And <u>don't</u> take the Holy Name in my presence! – Have a little respect!

PAMELA: Goodness gracious me... do have a care for your blood pressure, Cousin Hanna...

Julia appears at the kitchen door, also in her party clothes. She looks ethereal and radiant.

Both Pamela and Hanna look mildly uncomfortable, having been surprised in a confrontation. But Julia doesn't notice...

JULIA: Ah, Hanna, dear .... You're up late...Did we disturb you?

HANNA: These summer nights. The birds make such a chatter... I'm glad you're safely home. I'm back off to bed now. Don't be too late Julia. You'll ruin your good looks with late nights... Goodnight to you. *(She looks at the clock.)* And good morning...!*(She goes.)*

Pamela emits something between a snort and a giggle. Julia makes a slightly wide-eyed face, but smiles.

JULIA: Dear Hanna. Ever vigilant over our well-being! You mustn't tease her, Pammy! She's kind.

PAMELA: What a scold! How can you bear her!

JULIA: Ah, she's a good soul. My mother was fond of her. Wasn't it a wonderful evening? Just wonderful. Never tasted such fine champagne.

PAMELA: You never flirted so much either!

JULIA: Me? A respectable married woman?

PAMELA: No man is safe! Even Dempsey came under your seductive radiance!

JULIA: I don't know what it was….every now and then, you just feel this enchantment….!

Echo of dance music in background: maybe Cole Porter's "Dancing Cheek to Cheek", which begins…"Heaven…"

JULIA: God forgive me, but maybe it's because we know the world out there really is so dangerous, and everybody's teetering on the brink, and there's a feeling of ….sort of heightened excitement and…and….sensuality.

Oh, God, I know we shouldn't be enjoying ourselves with all these terrible things happening! But maybe we've been given these moments of ….intensity…. because they won't come again.

PAMELA: That's exactly it! We have a short spell of gaiety in the middle of a vale of tears! Grab it! Savour every moment. Think of it as an eternal Irish summer – and the outside world so far, far away…with the birds at singing at two o'clock in the morning. And the dancing. And the laughter. And the champagne. And the music. And…the sheer sex-appeal of it all!

JULIA: If only …if only you could catch moments in your life, and bottle it up, like a perfume, and keep it for always, to stay with you whenever unhappy times come….

PAMELA: If only we didn't have to grow old! If only…!

Here – have a drink of the new cocktail I've invented. Spanish brandy and red lemonade. I've christened it "The Emergency".

JULIA: But life itself is the exilir!

Pamela hears her husband calling her from upstairs and goes out towards the staircase calling up to him...

PAMELA: Yes, darling, we're here....Julia's making tea...We'll be with you in a moment.

Julia is putting the kettle on...

JULIA: *(repeating).* Life itself is the elixir!

Dympna appears at the door, freshly awoken from sleep and clutching one of her dolls.

PAMELA: *(Continuing).* Oh, who do I see, who should be tucked up in their little bed!

JULIA: Dympna! Are you all right?

Dympna goes over to her mother and hugs her.

DYMPNA: Had a bad dream, Mamma! A big plane came over our house and bombed us all!

JULIA: *(Tenderly taking up the child.)* Sure, don't you know that could never happen! We're safe! We're safe and everything's just fine!

Music. Ends Scene 7.

SCENE 8

1984. The care home, Dalkey, south Co Dublin. Julia is sitting with her back to the audience, looking out the window. Gemma enters quietly: she is carrying a tape recorder. Both mother and daughter are dressed in their signature colours – the purples and lavenders, the orange, saffron, brown....

Julia swivels around in her chair. She is more lucid today.

JULIA: Do you know what I'd like now, darling?

GEMMA: *(Kissing her.)* Anything in my power, Mamma.

JULIA: A piano.

GEMMA: A piano?

JULIA: Yes. A piano. A pianoforte. You know: a keyboard you play. It makes music. They call it "tickling the ivories".

GEMMA: Ah, a *piano.*

JULIA: Yes, darling. Look – am I senile, or are you?

GEMMA: You're not senile, Mammy,... you just have...lacunae of memory and recognition...

JULIA: Oh yes. And whatever you're having yourself.

GEMMA: You're as sharp as buttons today!

JULIA:	Knives.
GEMMA:	What?
JULIA:	Buttons aren't sharp. Knives are sharp. "Sharp as knives." *Comme les couteaux.*
GEMMA:	God almighty, you're amazing, Mammy, today!
JULIA:	It's the drugs talking. They have me like some class of a dope addict in here....
GEMMA:	Well, I've got a tape recorder here. It can play music tapes.
JULIA:	*(wailing.)* But I can't tickle – or tinkle - its ivories! I want to <u>play</u> the piano. Oh, your father loved to hear me playing the piano. "We'll Gather Lilacs in the Spring Again." That was his favourite...
GEMMA:	I'll ask Mrs Brady if we can have a piano moved in here. I can't see why not.
JULIA:	*(mimicking, skittish).* "I'll ask Mrs Brady if we can have a piano..." God almighty – there was a time we didn't have to ask the servants for permission to play the god-damned piano!
GEMMA:	Mammy! Your language! *(More in astonishment than disapproval.)*
JULIA:	Blame the films. Or the TV. The films that do come out of Hollywood! "The divil's own invention," poor Cousin Hanna used to say. Do you remember Cousin Hanna, *a storeen?*
GEMMA:	Only very vaguely...
JULIA:	Ah, she died when you were young....Stroke. Very

religious. But devoted to Dympna. She gave Dympna a great love of reading. I'd never have had the patience. Parties. That's all I wanted. Come here to me, darling, for a moment, will you?

Gemma approaches her face to her mother's. Julia examines it.

JULIA: Darling – do me a favour: put a bit of rouge on your face! You look so waxy! I can give you the money for a bit of Max Factor....*(searching for handbag.)*

GEMMA: It's fine, Mammy, it's just fine. I bought some rouge: I...just haven't had time to put it on...I'm going to: I'm going to...

JULIA: All right – but do, won't you? It's very important at your age. And don't let your looks go....

GEMMA: Mamma – more important - I've got this little tape recorder here, and I'm going to record some of your memories ---- only the happy ones. Okay?

JULIA: Do you go to Mass, darling?

GEMMA: Well....if I can....sort of...

JULIA: It's different on the Continent, I know. Your father said to a French friend – "but Pierre – why do you not go to Mass each Sunday?" And the Frenchman said..... the Frenchman said.... "Je suis Catholique: mais je ne suis pas fanatique!" That was a good one, wasn't it! "Je suis Catholic – je ne suis pas fanatique!" *(She laughs uproariously.)* They thought they were doing well if they went to the chapel at Christmas and Easter!

GEMMA: You haven't forgotten a bit of your French.

JULIA: You don't forget anything you learn before the age of

24. Before 24, it's written on stone: after 24, it's written in water. Who said that? Someone or other. Ah -- "They are not long, the days of wine and roses." Byron.

GEMMA: No, Mother – Ernest Dowson...

JULIA: Never heard of him...

(Gemma has the tape recorder working.)

GEMMA: Now tell me more about who taught you French. You had this very enlightened nun, at your school, didn't you...

JULIA: Mother Scholastica. Brilliant. Brilliant. One day, another girl dared me – she said – "Julia, you're got the nerve – why don't you ask her why Oscar Wilde went to jail"?

            "Well, I said, I suppose Oscar Wilde must have been a Fenian..wasn't that why Irishmen always went to jail in England?"

            "No, no, she said – she was called Bernie O'Malley, long fair hair – it wasn't that. It was something else. It's a terrible secret. Ask."

JULIA: *(continuing)* "So, up I get, in front of the whole class, and says I – Mother Scholastica – why did Oscar Wilde get sent to jail?"

            Well, Scholastica turned around, as cool as a cucumber, and looked me straight in the eye and said – "oh, just for loving another man".

            She made nothing of it at all.

            God she was enlightened. Before her time. Now our

62

own Mother would never have said that. Mother was
very prudish. Oh, and against drink. "Ireland sober
is Ireland free." The Gaelic League. Sinn Fein... as for
smoking cigarettes! Out, out, out.

Sometimes I long for a cigarette still.

GEMMA: I wouldn't object to one myself.

JULIA: Sure, you have to die of something. I have had my
           moments. You can have your years.... Well, I'll smoke
           again when we return to live in Monticello. In April,
           we'll drink a lot of champagne.
           *Rosie appears, with various medicines, and a filmy
           violet scarf, which she goes over and drapes around
           Julia's neck.*

ROSIE: Now! Don't you look pretty! Doesn't she look lovely,
           Gemma?

           Gemma smiles appreciatively.

JULIA: Sure, I'm fit for a ball now. Where's the ballgown?

ROSIE: *(winking at Gemma.)* I'll be up with that presently. Oh,
           you've got the recording yoke. I won't interrupt you so.
           Just brought your medicines, Julia.

JULIA: I'm stuffed with medicines. Ye have me drugged up to
           the two eyes.

ROSIE: Yeah, but you're much better than you were.

JULIA: Am I? Do you mind the days when you were bringing
           me champagne cocktails...[*"Do you mind": country
           Irish colloquialism for "do you remember?"]*

ROSIE: Ah, now, they <u>were</u> the days...

63

JULIA: Wasn't your poor father killed in the Great War, Rosie?

ROSIE: No, that was my grandfather, Julia. Me Ma was
            very attached to him. She always wanted to go out to
            Belgium and visit his grave.

JULIA: Didn't I see the Dublin Fusiliers marching around
            St Stephen's Green before going off to Flanders?
            We watched them from the dormitory windows in
            school. They were singing as they marched. "Are
            we downhearted? No!" And "It's a long way to
            Tipperary." God help them, they were all so laughing
            and bright. *(Her voice goes tremulous.)* Sure, they were
            all blown to smithereens. There was a little drummer-
            boy from Wexford: he was only 14. All blown to
            smithereens. "The war to end all wars." <u>Mar *dheadh*</u>.
            *[Ir: "as if to say": denotes sarcasm: pronounced "marr
            yaah".]*

            Rosie is busying about – perhaps watering a plant.

ROSIE: Oh, your sister-in-law Meg was on the phone, Julia.
            She'll be popping in to see you later. I'll leave the
            medication on the side – you won't want it for another
            while. *(She slips out unobtrusively.)*

JULIA: *(gazing out of the window).* That was why so many
            people were against the Second War. The First War
            turned out to be such a cod. When we were in Nice on
            our honeymoon...all over France, so many widows,
            dressed in black, like crows. So many mothers
            mourning sons.

            So many million men lost. All for a few feet of ground.
            I remember that so well. Your father was a pacifist,
            darling. War never solved anything, he used to say.
            And then all the troubles here in Ireland in the 1920s.
            Shootings in the street and then the Black and Tans.

The country was in a shambles. Sure everyone wanted peace.

But that wasn't the whole story.....it never is....*(fading a little)*.

Julia seems to be in a reverie for a moment or two... Gemma leaves the tape recorder running but goes out to a balcony where she lights a cigarette. Then Julia comes back to consciousness with a jolt.

JULIA: I dreamed last night I was having a baby. The old people used to say that was a sign of impending death. Sure, you have to die sometime. "Welcome be the will of God," that's what they used to say, long ago. They were wise in their way. If you can accept everything in this life, then you are serene....

Gemma returns, cauterising the cigarette, but retaining the half.

JULIA: I was just saying – if you can accept everything in this life, you are serene. "Kismet." Nelson's dying words. They <u>said</u> it was "Kiss me, Hardy", but Mother Scholastica said it was "Kismet". "That is Fate". Accept your fate with grace...

GEMMA: Ah, we don't hold with that at all, nowadays. *(Half ironic.)* We're in control of our lives now! We believe in "choice".

JULIA: Yerra, you'll soon find out that man proposes and God disposes.

GEMMA: *(Examining the tape recorder to ascertain that it's still operational.)* So – Mammy – tell us – what did you feel when the Second World War broke out?

JULIA: That wasn't the Second World War <u>then.</u> That was
         "the Emergency...."

Darkness. Music. Ends Scene 8

SCENE 9

Suggest here a sort of bridging visual interlude. We see a picture – perhaps a projected photograph or image - of the old family home, "Monticello", with a willow tree in the front garden. We see it through the changing seasons and the years, and through certain processes of modernisation, from the 1940s to the 1980s, with, finally, its amalgamation into a hotel.

The scene to be accompanied by a medley of popular music reflecting the changing times.

Gradually, the picture of "Monticello" fades...leaving only the cries of seagulls in the background.

Ends Scene 9

SCENE 10

September 1940.

Pamela Hart-Callaghan's home in Dublin. An impression of upper-class ostentation. No one on stage at first. We hear the yapping of a little dog. Then a radio is turned on, and some pips are heard.

FEMALE
RADIO
ANNOUNCER: <u>*Dia's Muire dhibh a cairde.*</u> *[Ir: standard greeting for Good Day: literally, "God and Mary be with, o friends." Prounouncing guide: Gia iss mwirrah yeev, a kordya.]*

Here is the news on Wednesday, September the Third, 1940. *(Announced slowly, plainly and with as much "neutrality" as possible in the voice.)*

In further measures to cope with The Emergency, Mr De Valera announced that ration books and gas masks will be distributed to all.

The harvest has been good this year and milk yields are on the increase.

The singer, Mr Bing Crosby, has paid a visit to Rineanna Airport in the Shannon region and was welcomed by local dignatories.

RADIO
ANNOUNCER: *(Continuing)* Hostilities over the English Channel have been reduced. The so-called "Battle of Britain" is

68

said to be over. London is braced for what is known as "blitzkrieg" bombing.

In Rome, Signor Mussolini has had a meeting with Herr von Ribbentrop to discuss Africa.

Japan has signed a pact with Italy.

Mr De Valera has encouraged all able-bodied men to join the National Defence Forces. There are expected to be more delays on all trains, owing to fuel shortages.

RADIO
ANNOUNCER: *(Continuing).* With travel now prohibited outside of Ireland, except by special permission, the Irish Tourist Board has commenced a programme of promoting holidays at home.

A new cinema has opened in Dublin. It will show a motion picture starring Miss Judy Garland and Mr Mickey Rooney....

Fades.

Lights up to reveal Pamela's fussy bedroom, with a bathroom en suite. Pamela and Julia are sitting on a sofa, smoking,and looking concerned

PAMELA: You can't be, Julia, my dear. You just can't be.

JULIA: *(Palpably miserable.)* Well....maybe I'm not. I keep hoping....Miracles happen.

PAMELA: It's preposterous. It's totally preposterous.

JULIA: I've been codding myself into thinking that maybe it's the change of life....

PAMELA: Don't be absurd! You can't have the change of life at 42.

JULIA: My mother had it in the mid-forties....I've heard of it happening at 40.

PAMELA: Oh. Well if it happened to your mother, perhaps so.... Why don't you see a doctor about it?

JULIA: *(miserably again.)* Putting it off.

PAMELA: Your brother's a doctor, isn't he?

JULIA: Pamela! You don't understand!

PAMELA: All right. Let's be sensible. Do the sums. How long since you've had the curse?

JULIA: I wouldn't call it a curse if I saw it now! ....Must have been May... The day we were having tea in town, and we heard about Holland and Belgium.....soon after that. Must have been early June.

PAMELA: July. August. September. Three months...

JULIA: I didn't notice at first....I swear I thought it might be part of the change of life..... I didn't think anything of it. But now I'm having other symptoms... You know.

PAMELA: Do stop beating about the bush, Julia!

JULIA: Well, God knows you know enough about sex – you should know all about the symptoms!

PAMELA: Oh, don't lose your rag! It's not <u>my</u> fault!

JULIA: I'd say it <u>is</u> your fault, Pamela Hart-Callaghan! *Pamela is open-mouthed.*

PAMELA: How in heaven's name does that come about?

JULIA: *(Confused, distressed.)* Oh, I don't know....All your fine talk about .... How we should mingle with men *(imitating her)* and absorb masculine <u>auras...</u> coming from their armpits.....That's what did it.
All those ferry-things...got all jazzed up. And <u>I'm</u> the one who pays!

PAMELA: *(Helping herself to a gin and tonic.)* Pheromones. Would you care for a gin and tonic?

JULIA: Ugh! The very thought makes me sick.

PAMELA: Well, you won't mind if I do...let's think rationally about this. After all, you haven't been pregnant for over ten years ----

JULIA: I hate that word! I hate it! It's what they say about beasts, down the country. "The cow is pregnant."
Worse.
"The sow is pregnant." Disgusting! Animal! Cattle and pigs – that's all it's fit for!

PAMELA: Well, reproduction <u>is</u> an animal function ....what I was saying, dear, is that since you haven't been, shall we say, <u>expectant</u> for over ten years – it's rather unusual to be expectant now. Particularly since you've only two children anyway.

JULIA: What's that got to do with it?

PAMELA: It indicates you're not very fertile. Not like all these unfortunate poor-class wretches who have twelve or fourteen children. Of course, your husband has had to be away quite a bit – so I suppose that's got to go into the equation. Unless you secretly had a a lover – that you never told me about!

A pause. Julia snivels.

JULIA: What do take me for – a harlot?

PAMELA: An affair can be very good for a woman. It stimulates all those pheromenes...

JULIA: Oh, you would know about having affairs! Madame Wordly-Wise! You've been shrewd enough never to ....have to face the consequences.

PAMELA: Don't be so unsophisticated, Julia. It's not getting us anywhere.

JULIA: You don't understand Ireland, Pamela. You don't understand..the mentality here...the Irish sense of morality....

PAMELA: You might be surprised what goes on in Holy Ireland. Tim hears some pretty hair-raising stories from his *gardai...[Ir: Police. Pronouncing guide: gardee.)*

JULIA: *(Wailing.)* My youth gone, gone! The very, very, very small chance of a few years enjoyment --- all gone! All right - I'll have a drink of lemonade, or tonic water or something. Put a finger of gin in it, then.

           They are both silent for a moment, as Pamela gives Julia a drink. Pamela mixes herself a stiff gin and tonic.

           Julia walks around, agitated. Pamela watches with drink and cigarette in hand...thinking.

JULIA: I was completely and totally confident that my childbearing days were over. 42 years of age! Ten years of normal married life, without a shadow! And now... this! I can't bear it! I can't bear the thought of having another child at my age!

PAMELA: Well, you once told me you had a miscarriage before
            Ignatius was born. Maybe you'll have one again.

JULIA: *(Putting her hands together as if in prayer.)* Yes –
            please, God! Please!

PAMELA: How did it happen – this miscarriage?

            Julia puts the drink aside, making a face.

JULIA: Ugh, gin…. I was hanging up some curtains, and I
            climbed up this ladder….Then, I sort of lost my footing,
            and fell down…Then….I had a little show of blood…
            and a day later, the pregnancy… sort of, came away. I
            passed it in the toilet….It looked like a small chicken….
            That was that. After a few days, I was fine.

PAMELA: You could always try hanging up some curtains again.

JULIA: Then I might break a leg or an arm…..Could try
            getting up on a horse. Horse-riding's supposed to make
            women miscarry…*(Wails again.)* I don't like horses! I
            only like donkeys!

PAMELA: We could explore other measures…But you have to be
            sure, Julia…You have to be sure that you are sure of
            your condition.

JULIA: *(Passionate.)* I'm sure…. I'm sure….And I'll try
            anything. I really really don't want another child.
            When the truth began to dawn on me – oh, I can't
            explain – I felt so trapped! So trapped! God forgive me
            – I feel like drowning myself on Sandymount Strand…

PAMELA: *(Drily).* You can't drown yourself on Sandymount
            Strand. The water's too shallow. Try Dun Laoghaire
            pier.

JULIA: Oh God forgive me. But if only, if only there was a way
            out....

PAMELA: Have you told Matt?

JULIA: Of course I haven't told Matt! You don't tell these
            things to a man until you have to! And of course I
            haven't told my brother either...that's why I haven't
            been to a doctor. I don't want anyone to know!

PAMELA: Well, we'll try something else, shall we?

JULIA: Nothing dangerous......Nothing that can't be explained
            as part of an ordinary accident... mishap. You're not
            going to take me to some murderous old crone who
            does things with dangerous implements....

PAMELA: You were talking about drowning yourself a moment ago.

JULIA: Oh, you *omadaun* – of course I didn't mean it.... but
            anyway that's not shameful in the same way as .....
            an illegal operation. I know a woman it happened to,
            Pam. It was terrible. We were at her funeral – she was
            supposed to have died from a burst appendix. And
            then, it went around the church in a whisper, that she
            had died from ------ *(whispering)* --- the results of an
            induced abortion. And one by one, everyone left the
            church.....The man ...who'd be the father of the child...
            afterwards hanged himself.

            It would be too awful for Ignatius and Dympna. And
            poor Matt! And my sisters and brothers! *(She dissolves
            into tears, half of rage, half of self-pity.)*

PAMELA: Pull yourself together, Julia. We are going to solve
            this problem. And no one will ever be any the wiser.
            (Suddenly firm, with her plan in place.) Do you hear?
            No one will ever be any the wiser?

74

JULIA: *(hangdog).* But I will be the wiser....

PAMELA: Now listen to me.   I want you to tell Matt that you
                and I are going to Greystones on Thursday – that we're
                going to an auction at the LaTouche Hotel. And that we
                may stay overnight with Edith...

JULIA: But why do we have to go to Greystones?

PAMELA: We're not going to Greystones. We'll be here. In the
                house. But Tim is away in the North for a conference
                and I'll give the maid the day off.

                She puts her arm around Julia.

PAMELA: Don't worry, Julia. Everything is going to be all right.
                We're going to solve this problem together, and you'll
                be absolutely fine...

JULIA: Oh God, Pamela – if only we can. It's the only thing
                I've ever been really, really sure of in my entire life! I
                can't, can't, can't have another child!

                Darkness. Plaintive Music. Ends Scene 10.

SCENE 11

1940. All action is off-stage. We see Pamela's bedroom again and the entrance to the en suite bathroom. Lots of water sounds. Julia is shrieking.

JULIA: Ouch! you're killing me! I can't stand this!
              The water is boiling, boiling!

PAMELA: You've got to stand it, Julia! Immerse yourself! Go
              on! Plenty of boiling water, and lashings of gin. Here!
              Drink up!

JULIA: I've already had three huge glasses of this bloody
              poison! It's desperate!

PAMELA: Yes, well, remember, you're desperate, darling, so
              knock it back. Think of what you've got to gain!

JULIA: Can't I have a bit more tonic?

PAMELA: It's the gin that does the job...

JULIA: *(Wobbley voice)* Oh please, God, please! I'll do the
              Galway Novena! I'll go to Lough Derg! Anything!

              More sloshing sounds.

JULIA: Ouch! Not more boiling water....this really is torture
              --- agony.

PAMELA: Not as much agony as the alternative... it'll soon be
              over...and then you'll be jolly relieved... Did you take
              the double dose laxative I got you?

76

JULIA: Yes, yes.

PAMELA: And?

JULIA: Nothing. Just diahorrea!

PAMELA: You're sure you didn't pass the little chicken?

JULIA: No, no, I didn't! There was no blood. And no chicken!

PAMELA: It's just a question of sticking with it...

JULIA: *(Moaning)* Aaarrrgh...!

PAMELA: And for this afternoon, I've made a reservation at Iris
            Kellet's for both of us. You get the friskey nag, I get the
            quiet one...

JULIA: *(Sounding inebriated now)* We're supposed to be in
            Greystones – remember?

PAMELA: I've made the booking under false names...

JULIA: I hate horses! I only like donkeys!

PAMELA: More gin! And then, you're going to jump down
            the stairs, four at a time! We're going to get this job
            done, Julia, you and I .....Think of it, as our very own
            emergency!

            *Tipsey laughter, wails, gushing water, and background
            war sounds all mixed up, fading out on 1940s music.*

            *Fade Scene 11. Darkness for some moments to indicate
            a passage of time...*

77

SCENE 12

Christmas 1940. Carol music played by organ. Hushed church background, a stained-glass window. Presently, the sound of a confessional box sliding open.

JULIA: Bless me, father, for I have sinned. It's... it's some months since my last confession.

(We hear murmuring in response, but never actually hear the priest's voice.)

I committed many venial sins and failings in charity this year....*(Pause)*....This is my Christmas confession.

Pauses between each sentence now.

But there's another reason why I'm here today, Father. I'm ....I'm expecting a baby... *(Priest's murmur.)*

The child is due to be born in the spring ....*(Congratulatory murmur.)*

Well, I did not welcome this event, Father. *(Pause, distressed.)*
I did not welcome it <u>one bit.</u>

I'm 43 years of age, Father. *(Now speaking more quickly.)* I have two children aged 14 and 10. My husband is 65 years old. His business has gone right down because of the war – he is an agent for import-export, especially to France and Germany a....and the Emergency has just about left us high and dry.
I don't know how we're going to manage.

(More murmuring.)

JULIA: *(Continuing.)* It's all very well to say that, Father, but ...God <u>doesn't</u> always provide..*(with mounting distress)*....and I'll be a laughing-stock in front of my friends. Women of my age in this condition*!*

Pause.

And you may say I'm being selfish, but I just don't want another child --- I feel I have enough responsibilities --- and I just want to --- be a little freer of so many home worries all the time...

Pause.

There it is. I just did not welcome this pregnancy.
It's worse. I tried actively to get rid of it.
I had a friend who helped me --- she was very kind --- she saw how miserable I was.

We tried to ---- dislodge the pregnancy. We tried everything. Well, everything bar ....using instruments. We tried laxative, pennyroyal, vigorous horse-riding, bicycle rides, jumping downstairs....and endless gin baths....*(her voice breaks down into weeping).*
But nothing would budge it! Nothing!

Pause. Some murmurs.

Well, I <u>have</u> to accept it now. There's no way out. What can't be cured has to be endured.

I don't want to make a bad Confession, and if I die in childbirth – and my closest schoolfriend <u>did</u> die having a baby, of pre-eclampsia, which is <u>terrifying</u> - I don't want to die in a state of Mortal Sin .But it is hard to say I repent, because I did it all very deliberately. And if I

79

could wind back the clock, I would!

*A longer phase of murmurs. Julia gradually seems
more composed.*

Yes. Yes.
Yes, I'll try to think of Our Lady at the Annunciation,
and how she accepted what the Lord had ordained for
her....I'll try....

*Julia listens again, and seems more comforted by what
she hears.*

JULIA: *(Continuing)* That's a very comforting thing to say,
           Father. Very comforting indeed.   Yes, I'll try and look
           at it that way.....yes, yes, I know, yes, we must say yes
           to life: I understand that, yes......

           *Murmuring, as Julia begins her Act of Contrition,
           which accompanies the priest's absolution, fading...*

JULIA: "O my God, I am heartily sorry for having offended
           Thee...."

Sonorous music. Ends Scene 12.

SCENE 13

1984. Gemma's bedroom at the Argyll Hotel. The church window from the last scene somehow morphs into the old bedroom window that still remains from Monticello. Something in Gemma's body position seems like an echo of the Confessional in the previous scene – she may be leaning against the bed in semi-kneeling position.

The telephone rings and she picks it up....

GEMMA: Yes.... Hello....Oh, thank you for calling me back, Dr Conrad. Yes, it's been a while....I've been travelling a lot.

Pauses for response from her counsellor.

Yes, I'm in Ireland seeing my mother. Oh, I feel such a jumble of emotions...What's difficult is talking to her and keeping away from painful or difficult subjects. She talks about my brother quite a lot, but if I were to remind her that ...that he died...it would just bring the grief back all over again. That's what happened before: she'd forget, and then you'd tell her again, and it would just open the wound all over again.

GEMMA: *(Continuing)* And my sister, who's in South Africa, has been in trouble with the authorities there – she's a sort of radical nun, and she's been protesting against the Government and is under a kind of house arrest – so that's another worry, and hard to explain...

And the worst thing of all is that Mama wants to go back to our old home, and it's just not there any more....

So I certainly can't tell her that I'm thinking of leaving my husband. Although she's strangely instinctive about some of these things....

Pause.

And I'm now not so sure about leaving Carl. Yes, I know I desperately wanted to walk away .....But..... Being in Ireland....I'm actually staying in a hotel that was once my old home...it's somehow anchored me to .....relationships are important: you can't just give up on them that easily. I mean...

Pause.

Yes. I know, Dr Conrad. I have to affirm what I want, and make my choices. I know. I know. I have to be brave enough to ......affirm my own empowerment, I know. But it isn't always that easy. Maybe I'm not brave enough just to walk away, or maybe I am just making excuses, or maybe I don't want to be a lonely divorcée in my middle forties.....Maybe I'd like to have another child, after all. Maybe there is a path laid out for us all....

Pause.

In one way, I'd just like to give up my job, come back to Ireland and look after my mother. She's such a wonderful character.... I remember now how I used to pray, when I was a little child, that she and I would die at the same time, so that we would never be separated.....

That's all come back to me now. But also my difficult teenage years, when I thought she had such antediluvian attitudes to women's lives – that they had to accept fate passively instead of having confidence in their own choices... .....it was a real generation clash.

Yet it breaks my heart that she has had such a hard life...a life so full of disappointment and loss. She was so kind to people, yet many people let her down. She has had so much loss....The heart of the romantic is always bound to be disillusioned....

GEMMA: *(Continuing)* And still she represents to me something of the heroic symbolism of motherhood. Because she gave and gave and gave again...

Longer pause.

Well, yes, Dr Conrad, yes....that is a very positive way of looking at things. Yes, I will think of that, and it does help...

Pause again.

Yes, yes.... Yes I'll see you on the 10th of next month, as we arranged... That'll be good....yes....thanks...

Gradual fade to dark. Ends Scene 13.

SCENE 14

1984. Moments after the preceding scene. The lobby of the Argyll Hotel. Deirdre is on the telephone.

DEIRDRE: Yes, I see. Yes, I'll give her the message. All right, Mrs Brady. I'm sure she'll call you back. I hope everything is all right now: bye-bye.

Gemma appears, dressed in outdoor clothes.

DEIRDRE: Oh, Ms Fitzgerald – I tried to put the call through to your room, but you were engaged....A Mrs Brady called to say that your mother had an unexpected troubled night, and her breathing is not too good. *(Consults a piece of paper on which she has written the message.)* No need to be alarmed, she said, but she's getting the priest in to give her the sacrament of the sick, and she hopes to see you later....

GEMMA: Oh God – could you call her back and tell her I'm on my way...right now....here's the number....

(She goes to desk and writes it down, then fumbles for car keys....)

DEIRDRE: Oh, and I had a call last night from Mr Cunningham in Florida. I told him you were staying here and -----

GEMMA: *(Distracted)* Yes, give him my regards. And Eileen, too. Especially.

DEIRDRE: --- and he said that your mother was one of the "most charming and unforgettable people he had ever known". And when the new extension is opened, he'd like to call it – "The Julia Fitzgerald Annexe".

Gemma feels suddenly touched by a rush of mixed emotions.

GEMMA: Her little bit of immortality. God knows, she deserves it….

She rushes off, and Deirdre, remembering something else, calls after her.

DEIRDRE: Oh, and another thing ---- your husband phoned from France. He just called to say that......

She shrugs her shoulders.

Didn't hear. Maybe didn't want to hear…Strange lady!

Fade. Ends Scene 14
Music.

SCENE 15

1984. The care home. Julia's room – her chair has been turned into a kind of daybed. Rosie is holding Julia's hand, stroking it. Faint echo of "We'll Gather Lilacs in the Spring Again.." Julia is in that fitful mood of lucidity mixed with abstraction.

JULIA: Funny, I can still hear that music. (Feeble effort at singing.) "We'll Gather Lilacs in the Spring Again…"

ROSIE: We'll get that piano for you yet.

JULIA: Hardly worth it now…

ROSIE: Course it is…

JULIA: What became of all your brothers and sisters, Rosie?

ROSIE: Now you're asking. There's a fair clatter of them to account for…

JULIA: And the adopted children…

ROSIE: They were grand…And once they began earning, every Friday night, regular as clockwork, half the wage packet on the table for my Ma…

JULIA: She had her reward for a beautiful deed. Was one of them called Shirley?

ROSIE: How well you remember! She went to Australia. There was always a Shirley in those days, after little Shirley Temple…

JULIA: Dympna was mad about her. I feel as weak as a kitten.

ROSIE: Will I make you a cup of tea? Do you mind how I used
           to bring you the China tea in the Hibernian?

JULIA: China tea. So delicate...

ROSIE: I can smell it now. I heard that Mrs Hart-Callaghan
           died. She was called something else. Lady someone or
           other.

JULIA: Lady Coldstream.

ROSIE: You're as clear as a bell today, Julia, after your little
           turn last night.

JULIA: Change before death. Don't look alarmed, Rosie. I
           don't mind. I had a happy life, when all is said and
           done...And I want to join my darlings on the other
           side...

ROSIE: Lady Coldstream, yes. That suits her very well. Yes,
           there was something in the Evening Herald – about
           the former wife of the late Garda Commissioner....She
           was a strange lady. So English – and yet, no feelings for
           England during the war at all.

JULIA: She was herself.

ROSIE: I believe the husband was a very quiet man altogether.

JULIA: Quiet as a mouse. Completely under her thumb. We
           were great pals for a while, but later on, ah, she kind of
           dropped me....I went down in the world, Rosie. I had
           been a gay young wife. Then I was a poor widow. Sure
           Matt left nothing. Except a lovely, lovely memory...

ROSIE: Julia, it's love that matters, not what you leave...

Julia seems to doze off for a few moments. Then she comes back to life again.

JULIA: We had a cousin of my mother's living with us, Hanna O'Sullivan. She got a stroke and I looked after her, naturally. Twas a misfortune that she didn't make a will, because she promised to provide me with a little legacy. But, sure, she died intestate and all her nieces and nephews in San Francisco claimed her savings.... Not that I was after her money, but I could have done with it, with three children...

ROSIE: Come on, Julia, have a drop of juice, anyway. *(She lifts a cup to her lips, and Julia drinks.)*

JULIA: Then there was a very decent Jewess who was very kind to me. Rachel Wine in Wicklow Street. She gave me a part-time job in her dress shop, and clothes for half nothing...

ROSIE: *(Plumping up the pillows.)* Weren't you a great asset to her, with your colourful elegance? Sure you always looked so stylish!

JULIA: I felt such remorse then, about the war. The afflictions of those poor people – when you see the pictures of the starving creatures on the television, and the poor thin Jews in their striped prison clothes, God love them.... *(Emotional)* And us not bothering our barney about any of it, as long as Dev kept us neutral. Weren't we very narrow-minded, when you look back?

ROSIE: Sure that's always the way. You never seem to know what's right when it's happening. It's only afterwards you see anything clear at all.

JULIA: "Life has to be lived forward, but can only be understood backwards." Someone said that. I thought

88

it was Byron, but .... It's Danish. Was it Hamlet?

ROSIE: It's very poetic, whoever said it. Now – the colour's
           coming back into your cheeks. You'll be as right as rain
           by the time Gemma arrives...

JULIA: Little Gemma! I wanted to call her Florence, but
           Dympna insisted she had to be Gemma. Dympna had
           been the apple of her father's eye, but Matt was so
           taken with the new baby – we didn't want her to be
           jealous, so we said, "it's your new baby too, Dympna".
           And so she insisted on the name of Gemma...I hope
           Dympna can come back to Ireland soon...

ROSIE: Oh, she will, she will. Any day now, I'd say...Didn't she
           ring up last week? But she has her black babies to look
           after – a whole school of them....

JULIA: I shouldn't be selfish. She's doing God's work.

           Gemma enters, a little breathless...

GEMMA: Mammy darling! *(Goes over and gives her a very
           loving hug.)* How are you?

JULIA: "Big kith"! That's what you used to say as a child...

ROSIE: Sure, she's great now. *(Indicating Julia)*

JULIA: I'm great altogether! Change before death!

ROSIE: Your Ma was just saying you were to be called Florence
           when you were born!

GEMMA: Florence! Was I now!

           Gemma sits beside her mother.

ROSIE: Well – life is always full of surprises... I'll leave now, Julia, and I'll go and make a bit of a snack...and sure, by this evening, you'll be dancing the tango.

JULIA: The tango....wasn't that a lovely dance...the South Americans used to do it so well. Carlos Gardel ---- the Argentines would play that...

"God Bless the Child"... your father loved that one. Especially when you were born, darling-love...Did I dream, last night, that I was pregnant? That's a sign of approaching death.

GEMMA: No – you saw that on the television – it was all about Princess Diana's pregnancy....

JULIA: We never used to say "pregnant" in the old days. We thought it was only fit for cattle and pigs!

Ah, Baby Gemma! The day your father brought you back from the Rotunda hospital, after you were born... Brought you back in a jaunting car, showing you off all over Dublin. It was the happiest day of his life. He was radiant with joy.

GEMMA: That's a lovely story, Mammy...

JULIA: Radiant with joy. To have fathered a child again at the age of 66 ---- it was a symbol of life, it was a gift from God. He adored you...

GEMMA: I'll bring the tape recorder back later this afternoon, Mamma, and we'll remember more happy times...

JULIA: Sure, I mightn't be here this afternoon! *(Pause)* I might have a social engagement!

GEMMA: You might, and all, Ma!

JULIA: Sometimes the child comes --- "trailing clouds of glory", as Byron wrote.

GEMMA: Wordsworth, Mamma!

JULIA: Mother loved Byron. She would sit in a field of hay all day and read Byron, when she was supposed to be saving the harvest. How is Ignatius? It's a long time since he came to see me.

GEMMA: Tell me more about Grandmother's love of Byron.

JULIA: Tis funny. Byron was very shocking and yet Mother loved him, and her so prudish. Mother died before you were born. Pneumonia. They died of pneumonia in those days, and what harm...a gentle way to go. But she lived to see Ignatius and Dympna ...She loved Dympna....what about my grandchild? Haven't I a grandson? Sure, didn't you often bring him to me when he was just a little boy?

GEMMA: I'll bring him over to Ireland again soon. But he's at a boarding school now.

JULIA: Would you have more children? Sure, why not?

GEMMA: Sure, I'm getting a bit old for that now, Ma. And haven't I a career?

JULIA: Will you have that on your gravestone? "She had a career." Wasn't I forty-three when you were born? The easiest birth a woman ever had. Two hours labour. You just slipped out.

A long pause, as though Julia is in a kind of reverie. Gemma goes over to look out of the window. Then Julia speaks again, suddenly.

You know what the priest said when I went to
Confession, and I told him I didn't want another baby?

Pause.

He said – "Never mind, my dear. When you're old,
you'll be glad you had this child to comfort you." And I
am, Baby Gemma! I am! "Big kith"!

*Gemma goes over to her mother, and enfolds her in
her arms.*

JULIA: The day you were born, your father filled the room
at the Rotunda with daffodils and champagne. It
was a beautiful spring day and he was there to greet
the child of his old age! "Trailing clouds of glory...."
Monticello was filled with happiness and beauty....
Happiness and beauty.

*She sits bolt upright suddenly, her eyes unnaturally
bright.*

We were blessed to have you, Gemma, and he's
smiling at us now, in the morning light! Smiling in the
morning light!

Music.

End.

A State of Emergency

A Prose Afterword around the theme of Ireland during WW 2

(1) Author's note

(2) Irish wartime censorship — getting under the political radar

(3) Winston Churchill and Ireland

(4) "A queer little Irish peasant" — a profile of William Joyce, "Lord Haw-Haw".

(5) Five books examining Ireland during neutral times.

(6) Was Harry Patch right?

Author's Note

The moral fascination with World War II:

Like many people born in the 1940s, I have an enduring fascination with the period of the Second World War. After all, many of us born during this decade were born either into the war, after it, or indirectly, because of it.

Wars stimulate baby-booms for a number of reasons, from the dry demographics of the species' collective response for numbers lost, to the more human longing for continuity and attachment in times of urgency. Most popular songs during wartime are about home, love, family, and even the joys of domesticity ("and Johnny will go to sleep/ In his own little room again".) Wars and the dangers of wars also probably prompt more reckless sexual mores.

Ireland's situation as a neutral during the period of 1939-45 did not make it exempt from the great conflict, though our parents experienced it in a different way from the nearest neighbours, either in Britain or in Northern Ireland. (Or France, too, was always on the psychological radar of Irish Catholics: many of the clergy familiar to Ireland came from French foundations, and many of the saints we venerated were French: Bernadette, Therese of Lisieux, St Catherine Labouré of the Miraculous Medal, St Mary Margaret of the Sacred Heart.)

Yet that very neutrality makes the Irish experience of the Second World War in some respects especially interesting, if we accept a view put forward by Seamus Heaney that tolerating ambivalence is a kind of moral necessity. Even though I have often harboured strong opinions on a range of subjects, I find myself drawn to ambivalence, and the way in which life often works out quite the opposite to how we plan it.

The Irish experience of World War Two was ambiguous, ambivalent, mixed, varied, diverse, confused, the good, the bad and the doubtful all interwoven. Many are the comedic aphorisms that encapsulate these ambiguities: "I know we're neutral – but who are we neutral against?" (Winston Churchill thought this drollery very amusing.) "We want England to be beaten – a little bit." And the famous story about the Allied aircraft under German fire: the pilot is from Cork and the navigator from Tipperary, and while the bullets fly around their ears, the pilot shouts to his comrade – "One thing you can say for De Valera: thank God he kept us out of the war!"

People may do one thing and yet their actions are different from their value-system - an ambivalence sometimes more obvious in personal life. Many a divorcee has a strong commitment to marriage: many an old rake deeply disapproves of his offspring's profligate or promiscuous ways. Many a socialist sends his own son to a private school. This is sometimes called hypocrisy, but it can also be that aspirations do not always match action: and vice-versa.

In Britain, the nation was under threat, and from 1940, rallied for survival. In Ireland, the State imposed a rigid sense of neutrality, but underneath that, there were many different, ambivalent and complex attitudes. There were also, in Dublin, some Englishmen and women who had no admiration for the Second World War, who happened to find themselves in Ireland, or who choose to be in neutral Ireland.

This play is – in part - set during the most dangerous period of the war, for Britain, and inevitably, Ireland. During that summer of 1940 Hitler was within a whisker of crossing the Channel, and but for a change of tactic by Goering, who deferred "Operation Sealion" – the invasion of the United Kingdom - probably would have done so at the end of that summer. Ireland's fate would surely have been sealed, though in exactly what way was not known at the time. Some of those directing Irish political destinies worried as much about the British invading Eire (the 26 Counties of what is now the Republic of Ireland) as they did about the Germans. Strong republican elements thought Germany would "liberate" Northern Ireland from British possession.

"A State of Emergency" has elements of autobiography and of transmitted memory, but it also draws on social history research. It has weighed upon my mind and my imagination for at least twenty years: I wrote a first draft in the 1990s; I put that aside and wrote another version in 2006-7. And in 2009, having passed the middle of my sixties, I decided that now or never I must commit it, finally, to print.

The characters are half-observed, half-imagined: or half-remembered and half-invented. If the play has any value, they should stand as characters in their own right; but they also represent, to some extent, the variety of attitudes which were prevalent in the 1940s. History is often remembered through the interpretative lens of the present; even professional historians seem sometimes to judge the past by the standards of the present. In the annals of childhood, corporal punishment in the past is now called "abuse"; beating children certainly could be cruel, but it was considered a normal part of life, as a glance at the Billy Bunter comics will illustrate.

Anti-Semitism is, quite rightly, now condemned as hateful and unacceptable – partly because of what we now know about the horrors of the Holocaust. But in the 1940s – as I discovered when I researched British attitudes to William Joyce for my biography of "Lord Haw-Haw" – it was so ordinary it went unnoticed. British listeners to Joyce never even remarked on his anti-Semitic rants, because the mindset was as unremarkable as mother-in-law jokes, or grumbling about the Jehovah's Witnesses knocking on your door (or indeed, making jokes about Irish "bogtrotters"). This is awful, but it is the way things were.

The Second World War is now repeatedly described as "a war against Fascism"; yet it wasn't seen as "a war against Fascism" at the time, but, as adumbrated above, a war for survival. Winston Churchill, who undoubtedly inspired the British Empire to an extraordinary degree, had not been particularly critical of Fascism in the past; he thought Mussolini quite a good thing when the Duce first started up in the 1920s, and he certainly preferred Generalissimo Franco to any of Franco's opponents. So as far as the political picture is concerned, I have tried, as best I could, to represent attitudes (in Dublin) as they really were, even where that is now rather shocking to our eyes.

Some of what older members of my family told me about the Irish experience of the Second World War was bleak – the privations, the lack of petrol, the fear of invasion, the proximity to aerial bombing – but, as with other wartime experiences in the theatre of war, some stories alluded to an ambience of excitement and glamour.

Dublin was not short of parties, cocktail receptions, vernissages, the sparkle of the racetrack (racing being abolished in England for the duration), theatrical events, colourful spies drinking in the Gresham Hotel, Polish and German prisoners-of-war coming to blows in the streets of the capital, and later on in the war, gorgeous young Yanks popping down for wild weekends – and great Irish steaks - from their troop stations in the North of Ireland. There was, as Tim Pat Coogan has written, a sense of *huis clos* about the country: it was sealed off from the "outside world". But that is precisely the conditions for a drama.

Yet this is a story about a personal dilemma too – a significant personal dilemma which is not irrelevant to our time or to any time. When is the right moment to have a baby? What happens if one parent doesn't want a child, even if the other does? How are our decisions influenced in these matters – by circumstances, by friends? And how do we see things many years, or decades, afterwards? I have tried to be understanding about all sides of the dilemma.

Irish neutrality had an especially long-term impact on women, and on other social issues. In 1970, I was a founding member of an Irish feminist movement which campaigned for social change in Ireland - pertaining to the right of married women to be employed, to have financial autonomy, to have access to contraception, to serve on juries, among other issues.

Most of the changes sought in the 1970s had been effected in Britain, and in – most – of the other European countries because of the Second World War. Before the Second World War, most of the conditions restricting women's working and financial lives applied across Europe, and France, too, had laws prohibiting contraception (France didn't allow women the vote until 1945 – something achieved in Ireland – still under British rule - in 1918).

Generally, Irish women's lives before 1940 didn't differ greatly from the lives of other European women: but women's lives in Ireland didn't change because of the war as much as women's lives had elsewhere. It took thirty more years for such changes to have an impact. (Even wearing trousers was an unusual for women in Ireland until the 1970s, leaving aside lady golfers and equestriennes, often a dashing spectacle in their jodhpurs, in the *Irish Tatler and Sketch*).

In many other arenas, too, the Second World War affected Ireland more in the long term than in the immediate. There are great advantages to being neutral. Like Dympna, people wanted to be "safe". But for most benefits in life, there are also costs, personally and collectively: and sometimes, it is the other way about.

*   *   *

IRISH WARTIME CENSORSHIP

Getting under the political radar.

Neutrality in the Second World War was widely supported by the people of Eire. No observer disputes that. But censorship about the war – described, usually, as 'The Emergency' – was political, ludicrously strict, affected all media and was all-pervasive. It was so misleading about actual events as to be effectively mendacious.

It could also be personally unkind: Frank Aiken, the Irish Government minister who pursued the role of political censor with such zeal, would not permit parents who had lost a son to add 'Dulce et Decorum Est' to an austere death notice in the *Irish Times*, since the phrase went beyond the bounds of political neutrality. [*Dulce et decorum est pro patria mori* is from the Roman poet Horace: 'Lovely and honourable it is to die for one's country.' The implication is that Britain is the country for which one might die.]

An Irishman who had gone down in a naval battle had to be described as 'lost in a shipping accident' in the newspapers – which was considered an hilarious anecdote in Dublin café society, by the way. Movies such as Chaplin's *The Great Dictator* were banned lest offence should be caused to Germany's leader. Warnings were issued about 'anti-German gramophone records' and one of the chief censors, Joseph Connolly, even considered imposing some sort of censorship on toys and dolls.

Count Jan Balinski, who had links with the Polish Government in exile, was appalled by the severity of the political censorship he found in Eire, outraged that even Vatican broadcasts about the persecution of the Church in Germany and Poland were disallowed. Jazz, swing and crooning were also not permitted on Radio Eireann as being dangerous foreign influences: news broadcasts were strictly neutral. Photographs of Phoenix Park, Dublin, in the snows of 1943 were not permitted to be published in the newspapers as the censor ruled that this could be used as 'military information'.

Wars, even just wars, increase the power of the political classes. In Britain, many individual and civil liberties were suspended – private property could be requisitioned by the National Government peremptorily, rationing was imposed, evacuees were billeted on sometimes unwilling recipients and a State at war, on a command economy footing, becomes a kind of totalitarian State as the notion previlas that 'the man in Whitehall knows best'. In Eire, the political classes increased their power the better to guard the State's neutrality, which they did with great zealousness. By 1940, Catholic Ireland played second fiddle to political Ireland; sometimes the two coincided, but sometimes not.

Critics have claimed that Irish politicians were habitually too quick to bend their knees before the croziered power of a bishop; but in neutral Ireland, it was the politicians who were insisting that the bishops bend to them. Bishop Morrisoe of Achonry in his Lenten pastoral for 1941 made a moral point about the Continental dictators taking God from his throne and deifying brute force: 'We know that the Poles are suffering and we know how the Dictator has treated the Church in Germany...Can Catholics view with easy minds the possibility of a victory which would give brute force the power to control Europe and decide the fate of small nations? Thoughtless persons give no heed to these prospects, yet they may become very real'. The newspapers were forbidden to report this mild sermon and all appeals met with a blank refusal from Mr Aiken's department; when challenged about it, de Valera refused to concede or apologize.

James Dillon, the Fine Gael TD who was one of the few political figures in Dublin to oppose the wartime censorship – he was against neutrality and believed Ireland should have thrown in her lot with the Allies – took to publishing his own speeches in private and distributing them himself, which drew official ire; he was also disowned by his own party. James Dillon was a Catholic of the old Redmondite school whose anti-Nazi views came from a well-informed and morally developed conscience, but for his pains he was mercilessly lampooned and caricatured as a 'pro-British' shoneen (lickspittle). Only in the 1990s – years after his death – was Dillon reassessed as a heroic figure who stood publicly alone for what he believed was right.

This lack of essential information was to lead some people in Ireland, at the time, to see the nations at war as morally equivalent. Winston Churchill and Adolf Hitler were just two sides of the same coin.

Arland Ussher, a patriotic Irish Protestant who supported Eire's neutrality, nevertheless criticised not the neutrality itself but the indifference he observed towards Europe: it offended him as a European, he wrote. The Irish looked on 'with a cold eye' as the tanks rolled across Europe. The majority 'took no manner of interest in the war – or at most the detached and comfortable interest which one might take in a serial thriller.' Solipsistic nationalism designated the sufferings of other peoples to a lesser – and sometimes a competitive – status. If you mentioned the afflicted victims of war in Continental Europe, all you got by way of response, Ussher notes, was 'Kevin Barry's broken-hearted mother'.

If you alluded to the sufferings of the Poles or the Jews or the Czechs, all you got back was the cruelty of Cromwell. De Valera's own newspaper, the Irish Press, under the editorship of the ultra-nationalist Frank Gallagher, was keen to show that no people in Europe – maybe the world – had ever suffered as Irish nationalists had. 'There is no kind of oppression visited on any minority in Europe which the Six County nationalists have not also endured,' claimed the editorial in the Irish Press on 1 April 1943. Part of the nationalist agenda in Ireland has always been to keep Ireland's woes centre-stage and never to let the oppressor – England – forget her wrongs. But the wartime censorship – much stricter than in Sweden or Switzerland – enlarged ignorance of the conditions in Europe.

*   *   *

Yet, the political censorship office in neutral Eire was, effectively, bypassed by a most unusual source: the prayers and thanksgivings sent in by readers of the popular devotional magazine, the *Irish Messenger of the Sacred Heart*. [Its circulation was over 250,000 per monthly issue at this time.] Here the actual experiences of the Irish involved in the war were reflected and recounted: it got under the radar of the censorship, so to speak, since Mr Aiken's team thought that a religious magazine mainly aimed at women and young people was not important enough for their attention.

The editorial policy of the *Messenger* was to support neutrality – and initially to blame the war on human greed, vanity and racism. "Men worship money or seek after it instead of seeking after their eternal salvation. Or they worship their own bodies or their 'race' or the State,' it lectured in March 1940. There was a prevailing sense of gratitude that Ireland had been spared from this war. 'Amid the almost universal clash of arms, our own country stands apart, free, at least, from the greater and more direful result of war...Yet while we thank God for His goodness to us, the duty is incumbent on us of doing our best to help the victims of this terrible scourge as much as we can, both spiritually and materially.'

The *Messenger* had always been quite strongly nationalist, but it became clear from their readership feedback – readers wrote in both to request prayers, and to give thanks for favours received – that many of these were involved in the theatre of war, and might be depending upon the magazine as a form of spiritual consolation. This shifted the *Messenger's* viewpoint subtly: the faith took priority to all politics, and if Irishmen and women need the support of the faith during the conflict, they must have it.

Initially, the wartime censorship cast doubts over the freedom to publish letters mentioning the war explicitly, a concern expressed by the readers. 'I doubt whether you can publish this letter', said a 'Letter of Thanksgiving' in September 1940

'But I should like to offer my thanks to the Sacred Heart for many favours obtained. I am an Air Observer in the RAF and on numerous occasions I have been in tight corners during this war. However, I have always placed my trust in the Sacred Heart....I get and read the Irish Messenger regularly.'

Little by little, extracts from war letters began to reveal the true picture of neutral Ireland for many families: the State might have been neutral, and democratically supported as such, but many ordinary Irish Catholics were involved personally – and with the Allies. 'I was a member of the crew of a ship that was so severely bombed that she sank. Only six of the twenty-two in our department were saved and all these chaps were killed, not by drowning, but by bombardment.'

'I thank the Sacred Heart for the safe return of a young man from the war in France.' 'My nephew was saved from death by fire last week; it was a miracle.' 'Miscellaneous favours received: Safety during air raids. Safe return from Narvic. Safety of brother prisoner of war.' (Then, incongruously, thanks for 'prize won at debate'.)

Nearly all Irish families had relations living in Britain and there was much worry about air raids.

Between 1940 and 1942 the drama was continuous. Prayers and thanksgiving included: 'Safety of son in Royal Navy.' 'Husband missing in France. Prisoner of war in Germany.' 'During the Battle of France and the Battle of Norway, I promised the Sacred Heart I would publish my thanks in the Messenger if He would bring my brothers safely through both campaigns. He did.'

The active role of Irishmen serving with the Allies emerges through these anecdotes, with no prohibition from the censorship office. Thanksgiving for: 'Father only survivor of vessel sunk in South American and subsequently released from "Graff Spree".' 'Husband saved when ship torpedoed.' 'Safety of fiancé whose ship was torpedoed.' 'Safety of friend in Nay.' 'News of son missing in Greece.' Thanks for: 'Remarkable escape of my son when with the RAF in France last year. All his squadron, but he, were wiped out and with some refugees he escaped from Brest in a small boat. After some days they were picked up by a Dutch ship and brought to Plymouth.'

'When I joined the RAF fifteen months ago I prayed hard to the Saced Heart that I might be a success. I volunteered for Air Crew Duty and was accepted. Then I started praying for my "Wing" and my "Stripes" and after weeks of training I was successful in getting my "Stripes", a month later the "Wing" came along. I am now a sergeant observer and as I go on my flights at night my last murmured prayer as I fasten my parachute harness is Sacred Heart of Jesus I Place My Trust in Thee.'

Some of the letters and first-person stories describe the thrills of danger. In 1941 a 'grateful airman' described his experience of 'bombs falling all around me', of saying his Rosary 'while raiders were overhead', and still he came through.

Apart from the men (mostly men are mentioned) the *Messenger* reflected the experiences of those Irish people of caught in air raids in Britain itself. A Dubliner describes just coming home from England, and experiencing 'bad air raids' in Birmingham. From Tipperary: 'I return most grateful thanks to the Sacred Heart fo the miraculous escape of my brother during a raid on Coventry. Half of the house he was in was bombed, his half intact.' From Co Laois: 'I beg you to publish this letter of thanksgiving to the Sacred Heart for saving my daughter in an air raid in England. The house she lived in was the demolished by a bomb, and when she awoke she found she was the only survivor and escaped with only bruises on her legs.' Miscellaneous messages mention: 'Safety of relatives in England' 'Safety of Brother when ship attacked at sea.' 'Husband in Air Force granted leave.'

There were many, many messages of gratitude like these. The

mentality of the Messenger readers was an admirable mixture of the trusting and the stoical: if they, or their family, were saved from being bombed, drowned or 'machine-gunned' (in one example), they wished to express their own Te Deum, a natural instinct which has affected kings and commoners since the dawn of civilisation. But if they, or their relations, had met with loss or tragedy, they took that, too, as the will of the Lord: 'perfect resignation' was considered a cardinal virtue.

A Co Clare mother wrote of her grief thus: 'Over a year ago my son was killed in an RAF accident. He was a splendid specimen of manhood, full of innocent fun and deeply religious. One day he was in his workshop when a plane crashed into it, and he was killed instantly. They sent me home a Sacred Heart badge that Paddy was wearing, and although I did feel deserted by the Sacred Heart, somehow I got the grace of perfect resignation.'

Many, too, were the requests for grace to bear 'help in great sorrow' 'solace in grief'. And significantly, for neutral Ireland, the mothers – it was often the mothers – requesting prayers mentioned fear of 'the enemy', or 'enemy fire', not in terms of hatred or bitterness, but in terms of danger. It was implicitly clear that 'the enemy' was Hitler's occupation of Europe: there was no moral equivalence here between "belligerents" as the official Irish bulletins described Allies and Axis.

The Irish valued their neutrality: but deep down, as Tim Pat Coogan has written, people were not really morally neutral about the Second World War. The majority of Irish people knew that the Nazis were a bad lot – especially as the war wore on – even if they did not know the details about the horrors of the Reich. Yet, they didn't mind seeing England 'taking a knock'.

In another sense, Irish neutrality rather accords with a kind of fiction or ambivalence that that the Irish have been able to live with, and which Seamus Heaney says it is necessary to live with: you may maintain an intellectual or political position at one level, but at another, subconscious level, you know that things are seldom as they seem.

This is the famous Celtic circumlocution, as depicted by the intertwining circles of Celtic art: not thinking in straight lines but in an elliptical way, illuminating psychological truths. Ireland was theoretically neutral and even formally indifferent, but at another level, her people were frequently involved in supporting the Allies, and the intertwined constellations of family history were often more deeply significant than the outward political positions taken.

From Mary Kenny's Goodbye to Catholic Ireland. First published London 1997

*   *   *   *   *   *

WINSTON CHURCHILL AND IRELAND

Winston Churchill is such a universal brand today that he is quoted not just by historians or political commentators, but by entertainers like Sir Paul McCartney or the comedienne Joan Rivers, who allude to his well-known battles with depression – his "Black Dog". Ms Rivers – and Sir Paul – have often cited Churchill's aphorism about inner misery: "If you're going through hell – keep going!" And whole books about depression have followed the Chuchillian nomenclature, like Anthony Storr's excellent "Churchill's Black Dog" or Sally Brampton's account of her own depression – "Shoot the Damned Dog!"

Even in China, as Sir Clement Freud found, Churchill is recognised as a world name: Clement was once given a pokey little hotel room in Shanghai while his colleague, Winston Churchill MP, was allocated a very grand suite. The Chinese officials told Freud: "Mr Churchill had a very famous grandfather!" Sigmund Freud did not, in Chinese terms, rate on the radar.

However, there remains in Ireland a residual prejudice against Winston Churchill, who is regarded as "anti-Irish". This is a direct legacy of the Second World War period, when Churchill made wounding references to Eire's "skulking" in neutrality – a word that was never forgiven. (He believed that Ireland, being still part of the Commonwealth, was legally "at war – but skulking".)

That hurt Irish national pride immensely – as it was designed to do: Churchill was certainly incandescent about our neutrality because he believed it cost British lives and exposed British coasts. But it hurt Irish national pride, I think, because if there is one collective vice that the Irish have seldom been accused of, it is physical cowardice in the face of battle. Every British commander in the field has always maintained that "your Irishman is a fine fighting fellow".

Churchill knew this, and indeed he touched upon that point in a characteristically incisive speech in May 1945, when he said:

"Owing to the action of Mr De Valera, so much at variance with the temper and instinct of thousands of Southern Irishmen who hastened to the battlefront to prove their ancient valour, the approaches which the Southern Irish ports and airfields could so easily have guarded were closed by the hostile aircraft and U-boats. This was indeed a deadly moment in our life, and if it had not been for the loyalty and friendship of Northern Ireland we should have been forced to come to close quarters with Mr de Valera or perish for ever from this earth.

"However, with a restraint and poise to which I say history will find few parallels, His Majesty's Government never laid a violent hand upon them, though at times it would have been quite easy and quite natural, and we left the De Valera Government to frolic with the Germans and later the Japanese representatives to their heart's content."

This, too, met with a wounded reaction in Dublin, where it was interpreted as a classical example of English mis-understanding of Ireland's position: that it challenged the abiding belief which Irish nationalists had held dear, as even did moderate Irish Home Rulers – that Ireland was a sovereign nation, and that every sovereign nation had the right not to be invaded by a neighbouring nation, even if that neighbour were mightier.

On the other hand, Irish reaction was, arguably, a traditional Irish misunderstanding of Britain's defence position, and particularly, during the Second World War itself, how perilously close the British nation could have come to extinction: and how very alone Britain was in 1940.

The barb about "frolicking with the Germans and later the Japanese" was a Churchillian stiletto thrust against De Valera's public relations disaster of visiting the German Ambassador in Dublin after the death of Adolf Hitler.

The question of access to the Irish naval ports during the Second World War was a contentious one in Anglo-Irish relations.

In 1938, Neville Chamberlain was persuaded by Eamon de Valera to return the Irish naval ports of Cobh (formerly Queenstown), Berehaven in West Cork and Lough Swilly in Donegal to the Irish Free State. De Valera believed these naval ports were part of our sovereignty. Churchill thought that a great wickedness and a folly on Chamberlain's part: having been First Lord of the Admiralty, and obsessively interested in submarine warfare, he believed that Britain would need access to these ports in time of war. The historian Andrew Roberts has even suggested that the King – George VI – had the constitutional right to intervene to challenge Chamberlain's decision.

Churchill was convinced that not having access to these ports - because of Irish neutrality - could have put the outcome of the war in jeopardy. Irish historians are more inclined to emphasise the behind-the-scenes help that De Valera's administration gave to the Allies surreptitiously. And recent research is indicating that Eire was not, in practical terms, as rigidly neutral as had sometimes been claimed. It is also claimed that Churchill's judgement on the usefulness of the Irish ports was over-estimated. But he was right in saying that Northern Ireland saved their bacon: the port of Foyle, in Derry, was to prove crucial in the Battle of the Atlantic.

Churchill's verbal attack certainly caused great rage in Dublin, as there was a feeling that much surreptitious help had been given to the Allies – and fifty thousand Irishmen had volunteered of their own choice. After a few days, Eamon de Valera gave a controlled, measured and adroit response to Winston Churchill pointing out that might was not right, and it would be a poor outlook for international relations if such a principle were upheld. 'It is indeed hard for the strong to be just to the weak. But acting justly always has its own rewards.' Cleverly, Dev praised Churchill for not yielding to the urge to 'lay a violent hand' upon Eire. The Irish nation had 'never been so proud of him' [de Valera] wrote Longford and O'Neill about this response to the British leader. Churchill's subsequent electoral defeat was duly celebrated in Ireland with whoops of joy: and after the war, De Valera blamed Chuchill for the deterioration in Anglo-Irish affairs.

And that episode is still remembered by older Irish people, more than sixty years after the end of the Second World War. In the 21st century, I have still heard older people say that 'the one good thing about Dev was that he stood up to Churchill'. (This refers not only to De Valera's retort in 1945, but a famous radio speech he made in 1943, when he rebuffed Britain's offer of reunification of Ireland in exchange for participation in the war.)

In July 2009, the veteran correspondent from the Irish Times, Conor O'Cleary, spoke on BBC Radio 4 about his experience of reporting from Westminster, and how uncomfortable he had been in proximity to statues and portraits of Sir Winston Churchill, that "anti-Irish" figure.

But it is my submission that Churchill was not anti-Irish. He certainly was resentful of Eire's neutrality, and he certainly believed that not having access to the Irish naval ports was perilous. But Churchill was possessed of that driving urge to prioritise the defence of the realm, and perhaps, with his peculiar mixture of 18th century aristocratic entitlement, American resilience (for he was half-American), grandiloquent turn of phrase – "we shall fight them on the beaches" - passionate patriotism, and even the brandy and champagne with which he shored up his Black Dog depressions, he was, at that time, the unique personality to lead his country to survival, and finally, victory.

Yet Ireland should perhaps see Winston Churchill more in the perspective of his whole life, and his long record of recognising the Irish nation and its entitlement to nationhood: from the early years of the 20th century, he had been a committed champion of Home Rule for Ireland, at a time when many members of his class were almost religiously devoted to Unionism.

*   *   *

When I was growing up in Dublin I heard it said – erroneously, of course – that Winston Churchill had been born in Ireland, and when charged with this fact, had replied: "One may be born in a stable without being a horse." The same myth attaches to the Duke of Wellington, also erroneously. And to Lord Kitchener, born in Ballylongford, Co Kerry, though it is a more plausible application to him.

Winston Churchill was not of course born in Ireland – but at Blenheim Palace - but he did go to Ireland when he was just two years old,: his grandfather, the Duke of Marlborough was appointed Lord Lieutenant of in 1876. His father, Lord Randolph was Marlborough's secretary.

And Churchill writes affectionately about his very early memories of Ireland: and amusingly about how he nearly died from concussion when he was thrown by an Irish donkey, only nursed back to health by his ever-devoted nanny, Mrs Everest. He also picked up, in that childhood, the prevailing fears felt about the Fenians – at least by a ruling caste, and to some degree by Irish people of less vehement political persuasion.

Lord Randolph, Winston's father, is associated, in the Irish Republic anyway, with the Ulster Unionists at their fiercest. When visiting Belfast in 1886, during Gladstone's first Home Rule Bill, Lord Randolph famously reiterated the historic Orange cry of "No Surrender!" and declared: "Ulster will fight – and Ulster will be right." (To resist Home Rule). He is also remembered for coining the phrase, that when in doubt Tories should "Play the Orange card."

Later on, Winston sought to defend and explain his father's position, suggesting that "playing the Orange card" was more by way of a politician's gambit than a maturely developed policy. And Winston underlined some of Lord Randolph's positive attitudes to Ireland – he had been very encouraging about Catholic education, and he believed in extending the franchise to men of modest means. This defence of his father was, to some extent, motivated by filial devotion, since Winston always yearned for Lord Randolph's attention and approval.

Yet although capable of showing grace in personal dealings – he got along personally very well with Michael Davitt, the co-founder (with Parnell) of the Land League – Lord Randolph did believe, as a British Unionist, that "if we lose Ireland, we are lost". He was, in that sense, a committed Unionist and would not have sympathised with his son's Liberalism on Home Rule.

*   *   *

By 1904 Winston Churchill had joined the Liberal Party ostensibly over the matter of Free Trade, but it seems that his time in South Africa during the Boer War had also had a certain radicalising effect on his character. Despite – or perhaps because of – being captured and imprisoned by the Boers, he esteemed this feisty people.

Indeed, one of the more entertaining moments that Winston shared with Michael Collins in 1921 – during the Anglo-Irish Treaty negotiations - was when Michael said to Winston that "you put a price on my head! You hunted me day and night!" Winston then fumbled in a bureau and extracted a portrait of himself, with a "Wanted" sign in English and Afrikaans. "You see, Mr Collins," Churchill said, "I too had a price on my head. But whereas the reward for finding me was a mere £25, the price we put on your head was £5000! How much more valuable you were than I!"

Ah, well, said Mick: you'd have to take inflation into consideration!*

By the Ulster crisis of 1912 – King George V was convinced that both Britain and Ireland were heading for a serious civil war – Winston Churchill was a fully-fledged Asquithian Home

Ruler. He said in a Manchester speech that "the flame of Irish nationality is inextinguishable". And in the same Belfast which had celebrated his father, Winston was pelted with rotten fish. In 1912, Edward Carson was threatening an Ulster Unionist rebellion against the Crown, by enlisting the assistance of the German Emperor.

In September 1913, when Ulster Unionists were beseeching King George not to put his hand to any bill of Home Rule passed through the Westminster parliament, Winston Churchill wrote to the King to say that although "Ulster has a case, and that if Ireland has the right to claim separate Govt from England, Ulster cannot be refused similar exemption from Govt by an Irish Parliament. But he [Churchill] strongly resents that Ulster should talk of 'Civil War' & do everything in her power to stir up rebellion before even the Home Rule Bill has passed, let alone before the Irish Parliament is set up'.

In a meeting with King George, Churchill said that "Ireland has been earnestly waiting for the fulfilment of their dream for the past 30 years. Is it likely that she can now stand by & see the cup, almost at their lips, dashed to the ground?" King George's own private sympathies were more naturally Unionist, but he had a sense of conscience about doing the right thing, and acting fairly, and Churchill's counsel on the justice of Home Rule weighed with him.

Although he once said that "a foolish consistency is the hobgoblin of little minds" - Churchill was generally consistent all of his life in this: he did believe in self-government for Ireland: but self-government subject to the Imperial parliament. He was, after all, a British Imperialist, and proudly so: he believed in the Empire long after most other British statesmen had given it up. He also believed that Britain – indeed England's – security required that Ireland should not be a weak link in the western defences. But as a student of history, Winston was well acquainted the long Irish rebel tradition that "England's difficulty is Ireland's opportunity".

As we know, Home Rule was put on the back burner by the declaration of war in 1914. And in the middle of that First World War, came the Easter Rising in Dublin of 1916 which has become the founding legend of the Irish state. I think, rightly, the events of 1916 are now seen as not something apart from the Great War, but very much part of the same zeitgeist - of the nationalism of small nations breaking up from great empires – the Hapsburgs, the Ottomans, the Czarist empire.....

At the end of that war, Winston became Colonial Secretary in Lloyd George's Coalition, so he was to play a key role in the turbulent years that followed. And here, again, his reputation remains controversial. Tim Pat Coogan, biographer of De Valera and Collins, still refers to Winston Churchill as "the man who sent the Black and Tans to Ireland." Legally, they were despatched by Sir Hamer Greenwood, the Canadian-born Chief Secretary for Ireland, but Churchill certainly contributed to the idea of this militia, who behaved so badly that King George V himself said they should be disbanded and brought home.

On the other hand, there is little doubt that Winston's crucial support of the fledgling Irish Free State – and his continuing trust of Michael Collins personally after they had signed the Anglo-Irish Treaty together – made him, to some degree, the midwife to an independent Ireland, initially a Dominion with the same status as Canada and Australia.

Churchill could never accept the idea of an Irish Republic (at least until the end of his life) because he felt it would be, in essence, hostile to Britain – and Irish Republicans certainly could be Anglophobic. But the more moderate Free State, drawn up in 1922, which accepted the Crown and had an Oath of Allegiance to the King was, to Winston Churchill, a legitimate state worthy of his support and in the civil war that ensued between Irish Free Staters and Irish Republicans, Churchill did all he could to back the legitimate Irish State.

As we know, Michael Collins, defending the Free State, was shot dead in August 1922. Shortly before he died, he sent what turned out to be a valedictory message to Churchill: "Tell Winston we could never have done it without him." And that was the truth.

It might be argued that the Free State might have been a failed state without Winston Churchill's active support – sometimes in the face of parliamentary hostility at Westminster, where there were calls for Britain to re-occupy the country. Churchill was barracked by the House for defending the Free State, and saying "I trust General Collins", as diehard Tories and Unionists called for the reconquest of Ireland. Piquantly, one of the few M.P.s audibly to back Winston in the House of Commons in the debates over the Free State was one Oswald Mosley.

During the Second World War, when Churchill felt at his most aggrieved with De Valera's leadership of Saorstat Eireann, he said pointedly: "Of course, Michael Collins was a man of his word." He clearly believed that Collins would have permitted Britain the naval ports in time of war: or at least he made that pledge in 1921. We cannot know the "what if" of this element of history.

Would Winston Churchill have invaded neutral Eire if he thought it necessary? He was capable of taking ruthless decisions if he felt that it was do or die – as in the decision to shell the French fleet at Mers-el-Kebir. But he was, apparently, given advice by intelligence sources that invading Eire would have been more trouble than it was worth, since 80 per cent of the populace supported neutrality: and that even many of the pro-British element would have resented British coercion.

Churchill was, it seems, ready to do a deal with De Valera over Ulster: a united Ireland in return for a pro-Allied Ireland. But that was rejected – a real sense of distrust prevailed.

This was perhaps illuminated by a minor broadcasting incident in 1943. The popular Radio Eireann programme Question Time – a non-political general knowledge quiz show, chaired by Joe Linnane – was transmitted from Belfast one Sunday night. Linnane asked a competitor, 'Who is the world's best-known teller of fairy tales?' The correct answer was 'Hans Andersen' but the contestant replied 'Winston Churchill'. 'The audience exploded in laughter and cheers – they were mostly nationalist in the hall,' recalled the broadcaster Maurice Gorham, 'but questions were asked in the House of Commons at Westminster, formal representations were made from Belfast, and it was a long time before a Radio Eireann team crossed the Border again.'

After the Second World War, the paths of Britain and Ireland diverged once again when Ireland was declared a Republic in 1948 – though quixotically, De Valera disapproved of the Fine Gael-led coalition administration doing so. Winston at this point was more focused on the new menace arising from the Soviet Union and the Iron Curtain, and in a very strange way the spectre of Soviet Russia effected a certain limited reconciliation between Churchill and De Valera, and they had a cordial meeting as in Downing Street in 1953: by then, perhaps, a question of all passion spent.

For, although Sir Winston had always opposed an Irish Republic, there was one aspect of post-war Ireland that he approved of: the Catholic Church ensured that Ireland was, in the Cold War years, firmly anti-Communist and opposed to "godless Bolshevism". If Ireland had posed a security threat to Britain's western and southern approaches during the Hitler war, it would surely stand firm against any onslaughts by Stalin's influences from the east.

In Roy Foster's brilliant - and entertaining "Paddy and Mr Punch" he recounts an unusually occult experience of Winston's, when he fancies that he has a of a sort of spiritualist visitation from the ghost of his father. Lord Randolph asks Winston how Ireland is faring in the later 1940s, and Winston replies: "They are much more friendly to us than they used to be. They have built up a cultured Roman Catholic system in the South. There has been no anarchy or confusion. They are getting more happy and prosperous. The bitter past is fading."

In fact, it hadn't altogether faded. Papers recently deposited in the Irish National Archives show that there remained some sharply critical views of Winston Churchill among Irish officials. But these archives also show a conciliatory approach from Winston Churchill himself.

In November 1948, Churchill met the Irish High Commissioner, subsequently Ambassador, John Dulanty in London: Winston said to him - "I still hope for a United Ireland. You must get those fellows from the North in, though you can't do it by force.

There is not, and never was, any bitterness in my heart towards your country." (He had known the extraordinary Dulanty since 1906, and there was a long friendship established between them.)

There was also a significant coda to Churchill's famous 1945 outburst against Eire, recently revealed in papers in the National Archives of Ireland. Randolph Churchill, Winston's son (named after the previous Lord Randolph) had a long conversation with John Dulanty in which he said that 'his father's reference to Ireland and the Taoiseach [in May 1945] was a piece of folly....His father was the first to accept it.' It was a kind of apology by proxy.

Randolph went on to commend Eamon de Valera's response as 'a masterpiece'. It was his own opinion, too, that 'partition was finished', and that people in England were 'sick of the Belfast Unionists peddling their prejudices about Westminster and there was a very general feeling that the partition of Ireland was wrong as a matter of principle.'

Winston Churchill believed in magnanimity after the battles of history. When a quarrel was over, with Winston, it was over. He also believed that when Ireland became more prosperous that would heal the wounds of history and make Anglo-Irish relations harmonious.

He also believed that Ireland should be re-united – not by coercion, but by voluntary choice which would bring about a peaceful unity. The Belfast Peace Agreement of Good Friday 1998, and the subsequent Referenda in both parts of Ireland endorsing it by large majorities did at least achieve one very important measure – that any future constitutional arrangements would be decided by democratic decision only, on both sides.

As Professor Foster has said, history is a process of endless revision, and the revisions will go on; the debate about whether a mighty power has the entitlement to invade a smaller country for reasons of defence continues to go on. Debates about Churchill will go on, because he is far too big a figure to contain his own contradictions: but as for Ireland, I have no doubt that his affection for a country in which he spent a formative part of his young childhood – and which he supported at a crucial period of its nation- building well outweighed his criticisms in time of war.

From a talk given by Mary at the Cabinet War Rooms, London SW1 on 15 January 2008: with added material from the Irish archives, and cited in Crown & Shamrock: Love and Hate between Ireland and the British Monarchy.

*The personal meeting between Michael Collins and Winston Churchill in October 1921 was the subject of Mary's play Allegiance, *performed at the Edinburgh Festival in 2006, with Mel Smith as Churchill and Michael Fassbender as Collins, directed by Brian Gilbert.*

"A QUEER LITTLE IRISH PEASANT WHO HAD MADE THE WORST OF HIMSELF"

: a portrait of Third Reich broadcaster, William Joyce, "Lord Haw-Haw"

William Joyce, "Lord Haw-Haw", was the last man to be hanged for High Treason in Britain, on 3 January 1946. His offence had been that he had given "aid and comfort to the King's enemies", and had assisted Germany "in her war against our country and our King."

Joyce had been a broadcaster for the Third Reich, and his radio commentaries had been disconcertingly successful: at one point, he attracted some 16 million listeners in Britain and Ireland. His radio call signal "Germany Calling!" was used by stage comics to elicit hilarious laughter and instant recognition: for, although Joyce's propaganda broadcasts were odiously pro-Nazi, nevertheless, strangely enough they touched the British sense of humour.

Joyce's trial, in 1945, was a media sensation. When he appeared in the dock, the writer Rebecca West described him as "a queer little Irish peasant who had gone to some pains to make the worst of himself." The outcome was controversial, for William Joyce was not, technically, British. He had been born in America – the son of a naturalised American – and had grown up in Ireland. He had, in 1933, made an application for a British passport, in which he had mendaciously claimed to having been born in the

United Kingdom. By this act, claimed the brilliant prosecuting attorney Sir Hartley Shawcross, Joyce had wrapped himself in the Union Jack: his value to the Reich was as a supposed Britisher.

William Joyce was a very odd character, difficult and aggressive, who grew up in Galway during the revolutionary early years of the 20th century. His father was an Irishman from Killour in the Lough Corrib area of Mayo; his mother was English, but her father had been a clever doctor from Co Fermanagh. William always liked to boast about "the Orange blood" which coursed through his veins.

The family had moved from Brooklyn in New York, back to Co Mayo, and then to Galway city. From an early age he witnessed political street violence. He was a clever, precocious but rebellious boy, and expelled from his Jesuit school, St Ignatius College, apparently for drawing a gun on a priest. (He also argued with the local Bishop, which was an uncommon liberty at that time). More disconcertingly, he attached himself to the notorious Black and Tans and narrowly escaped being liquidated by the local IRA. Aged 15, he fled to England where he enlisted in the Worcester Regiment, but was soon discharged for lying about his age. He attended Battersea Polytechnic to study medicine, but was also ejected from there for behaviour problems: the school records found him to be an unmanageable young teenager.

At 17, he received a serious gash across his cheek after an encounter with a political opponent at an election meeting. The scar remained livid throughout his life and the significance of the wound went deep: he claimed that a "Jewish Communist" had tried to kill him, and this theme became part of a lifelong and pathological anti-Semitism.

Subsequently, he attended Birkbeck College, London, where he gained a First Class degree in English Literature, and began to manifest a certain academic brilliance. He was a gifted philologist, a fine scholar in Anglo-Saxon and Old Norse. Politically, he was involved with the Chelsea Conservative Party. Small, almost dwarfish in stature, and vehement of argument, he could nonetheless be engaging: if he had not seduced a young girl of good family in Chelsea, he might have been nominated for a Conservative seat in the Royal Borough of Kensington and Chelsea. (To the end of his life, he carried around his library ticket for Kensington Library.)

Joyce was studying for a Ph.D., when he was smitten by Sir Oswald Mosley, leader of the British Union of Fascists. From 1933 until 1936, Joyce was a star speaker for Mosley; but in 1937, after the British Fascists began to lose ground, he was discharged from the organisation, with whom he had a paid job. He and John Beckett formed their own group, The National Socialist League, but it failed hopelessly.

Increasingly, Joyce was living a hand-to-mouth existence as a private tutor, when, in 1939, he decided to go to Germany. In truth, by August 1939, he was all washed up in Britain. He and his second wife, Margaret – a fiery redhead who had almost joined the Communist Party before she, too, was attracted by Mosley - took the boat to Ostend on 26 August 1939. He had probably been tipped off by the MI5 spymaster Charles Maxwell Knight he would shortly be interned – Maxwell Knight was another odd character who back in the 1920s had had Fascist connections.

Through a series of flukes, Joyce was introduced to the Reich's propaganda broadcasting organisation and in October 1939 found himself before a microphone. "Lord Haw-Haw" was born. The nickname came from a radio critic who described a broadcaster who "speaks English of the haw-haw,damn-it-get-out-of-my-way variety". Various broadcasters contributed to the Haw-Haw character, including Norman Baillie-Stewart, Wolf Mittler and Eduard Dietze, but finally it was Joyce who took the role, with a particularly memorable rasping tone.

His broadcasts could be threatening, scoffing, sneering, comical, satirical, impertinent and occasionally radical – he always criticised "the swells", and upheld "the workers". Goebbels issued the orders, but Joyce wrote the words. As he had an unrivalled topographical knowledge of Britain – and Ireland – he was able to mention specific places knowledgeably, and this developed into a myth of occult dimensions. It was believed that "Lord Haw-Haw" had said that one town would be bombed, another spared. There are still many anecdotes about Haw-Haw's prognosticians, most unverifiable.

On one occasion, he is said to have reacted to Mr de Valera's promise to "repulse" any attempt by Germany to invade Eire. Joyce commented jocundly that Mr de Valera would have no more power against the mighty German tanks than "the tinkers on the Ballygally Road in Tuam". This caused some hilarity in the West of Ireland: but it was the fact that Joyce knew exactly where the Travellers in Tuam, Co Galway, were encamped that excited such awe.

It was reported, anecdotally, that up around the Donegal coast, fishermen would cheer when Joyce reported that another British submarine had taken a hit. A cousin of mine in Connaught said lightly, "Sure we were all up for Hitler at the time." "Lord Haw-Haw" had many listeners in Eire.

Joyce always feared America's entry into the war, and after 1942, his star began to wane. But he had made his commitment to Germany – he even became a German citizen – and he stuck with it. He and Margaret were captured in May 1945, near Flensburg in Schleswig-Holstein. He had been given the identity of "William Hansen", but when he spoke to two British soldiers, his voice instantly identified him.

In London, Parliament hurriedly revived a statute of 1351 to ensure that he could be charged with treason. The trial began in the Old Bailey on 17 September 1945 and was over in three days. An appeal followed 30 October but failed, as did a final appeal to the House of Lords.

In prison, Joyce wrote many letters to Margaret, full of complex language and ironic puns. He was unrepentant about National Socialism.

He had been married twice, first to Hazel Kathleen Barr, by whom he had two daughters: secondly to Margaret Cairns White. His eldest daughter Heather remained attached to his memory while deploring his politics: in 1976, she had his remains transported to Bohermore Cemetary in Galway, where they were reburied near to the Atlantic Ocean where he had played as a boy.

There was a strange cast of characters who had both Irish and German links in this conflict. Norman Baillie-Stewart, originally a Scot, was one of the early broadcasters from Berlin who also claimed to be one of the first voices of "Lord Haw-Haw"; he served three years in prison in England for serving Germany, and after his release, in October 1949, was helped by Quaker charities to migrate to Ireland, where he settled as James Scott, married a Dublin girl, and had two children.

Francis Stuart, the Irish writer and son-in-law of Maud Gonne, whom William and Margaret Joyce had known in Berlin when he broadcast on the German Irish service, returned to Dublin in 1948, marrying his German companion, Madeleine, who had liked William Joyce, and thought him courageous.

John O'Reilly was another Irishman who had been friendly with Joyce in Berlin: O'Reilly had been a customs' official, a seminarian, a hotel receptionist, potato picker, an interpreter and a spy. He had led a group of Irish potato pickers from Jersey to Berlin at the start of the war. His father had been one of the RIC policemen who arrested Roger Casement, and his wife, dramatically, died at the hands of a back-street abortionist, Nurse Cadden, in a notorious Dublin scandal in 1956. John O'Reilly returned to Ireland and was buried at Dean's Grange Cemetary in 1971, on the same day as Dev's successor as Taoiseach, Sean Lemass.

Edward Bowlby was an Anglo-Irishman who had also worked alongside the Joyces in Germany. He somehow escaped prosecution – considered "small fry" – and chose to make a new life in Ireland after the war. He subsequently called himself Charles Bowlby and became a teacher at Aravon School in Bray, Co Wicklow, which was described as a smart preparatory school mainly for upper-class Protestants. Along with Sir John Maffey, the British diplomat, Bowlby founded the Leprechaun Cricket Club in Ireland, and died peacefully in 1959.

The Second World War had a cataclysmic political effect and changed the western hemisphere. There are many great dramas – and tragedies - associated with this war that began on September 3, 1939: and there are many strange, eccentric and quirkey stories attached to individuals whose war experiences were far from orthodox.

Based on MK's entry on William Joyce for Scribner's Encyclopaedia of Europe, with additional material from her biography "Germany Calling: A Personal Biography of William Joyce, Lord Haw-Haw".

Books in time of war

My family in Dublin retains a vivid recollection of neutrality in Ireland during the Second World War. It was, I think, in 1943 that Herr Hempel, the German ambassador, came to my parents' house for drinks. A charming and kindly man, my mother recalls. After the war, my mother was shocked to learn that Frau Hempel had been snubbed in Grafton Street: people who had accepted the Hempels' hospitality now turned the other way. How ungrateful and capricious is human society! Eaten bread is soon forgotten! But Mother, I protested when young, these people had been *Nazis*. Oh no, my mother replied, Herr Hempel was never a Nazi. Herr Hempel was a gentleman.

Useless, it seems, to explain that being a gentleman – having good manners and elegant clothes – is no bar whatsoever to fascism, but as it turns out, my mother was right. Eduard Hempel, Hitler's Minister to what was then Eire was not a member of the Nazi party - a matter of some personal difficulty for him, especially when so many of his staff of 30 people in Dublin were Nazis. Hempel was a career diplomat who, on Robert Fisk's evidence, behaved as well as he could in the circumstances. Unlike the Nazis, he did not wish, or try, to lure Eire into the war on Germany's side, and he deeply disliked the German spies who arrived in Ireland from time to time, often with somewhat farcical results, with a mission to make contact with the IRA. Overall, Hempel strove to keep the mischief-making to the minimum: he had perhaps less reason to entertain illusions about Germany's New Order than the more naïve Irish. (Hempel's children grew up in Ireland and his son is now an eye specialist in London.)

Nevertheless, the atmosphere of Dublin during that period as remembered by my family – the cocktail parties, the balls, the cosy, undisturbed bourgeois life protected by a rigid Government censorship from events in the outside world – illustrates the almost unbridgeable gap in thinking between the Irish of that time and the British across the water. Britain was fighting for her very existence. Churchill considered from the beginning that Eire was simply 'skulking' legally, while de facto being defended by Allied action, a notion that Nicholas Montserrat echoed in The Cruel Sea.

'They [British submarine personnel] saw Ireland safe under the British umbrella, fed by her convoys and protected by her airforce, her very neutrality guaranteed by the British armed forces....As they sailed past this smug coastline, past people who did not give a damn how the war went as long as they could live on in their fairy-tale world, they had time to ponder a new aspect of indecency. In the list of people you were prepared to like when the war was over, the man who stood by and watched while you were getting your throat cut could not figure very high.'

Yet for the Irish in Eire – 80 per cent of whom favoured Eamon de Valera's policy of neutrality – their detachment from the war sprung from a valid historical source. Historically, England's wars had never been seen to serve Irish interests, and historically, too, Ireland's sympathies had often been with England's continental adversaries; a victory for the Spanish Armada, for example, would have been seen in Ireland as a welcome triumph for His Most Catholic Majesty. Irish lives had before been lost in Britain's wars – without, it seemed, much benefit to Ireland. It is natural, and indeed perhaps even right, for the leader of a nation to consider, first, his nation's own interest, and in the light of history, it seemed to De Valera that Eire's interest was best served by remaining neutral. At one stage, in the early part of the war, it would have been of considerable strategic advantage for Britain to call upon Irish assistance, particularly in the use of the Irish sea ports for the refuelling of submarines, but in view of the policy of neutrality, such assistance was not forthcoming. Moreover, the continuing obsession with the partition of Ireland made De Valera even less inclined to oblige Britain in her hour of need: Churchill's offer to contemplate Irish unity in return for co-operation from Eire was not trusted by De Valera. For the British, De Valera thought, a united Ireland would remain 'a deferred payment.

Robert Fisk's large and detailed book chronicling the events of this time was a rewarding one for me. Fisk is not a historian who gives the reader the grand sweep of historical developments, but a painstaking journalist who methodically records every detail. The book's value lies not in its perspective, which is almost laconic, but in its methodical documentation of the Second World War in the Irish arena.

As with Irish history generally, the picture abounds with paradoxes: Ulster huffed and puffed a great deal at the beginning of the war about its eternal loyalty to the Crown, an avowal which impressed Churchill greatly. Yet when the test came, Ulstermen were rather more diffident about serving in the forces and despite Eire's political neutrality, many individual southern Irishmen joined the allied forces, and some five Victorian Crosses were awarded to southern Irishmen as against one in the north.

Were elements in southern Ireland pro-German? Yes, elements were – the extreme Republican and pro-IRA minority not merely thought that 'my enemy's enemy is my friend', but were indeed romantically drawn to the ideology of the New Order, which was tied up with crackpot fantasies about the Germans and the Celts being of the same Aryan roots – conveniently ignoring that in terms of racial sources, the English and the Germans are far closer. Although in 1938, De Valera not only favoured appeasement with Hitler, but saw Hitler's actions in the Sudentenland as justified – he even considered appealing both to Hitler and Mussolini to explain Ireland's own need for *lebensraum* - in Ulster. Yet as the war progressed De Valera must have seen what the German Helmut Clissman adumbrates here – that Hitler would have disposed of Ireland just as he had disposed of Holland and Belgium, though he had formerly used folklore and nationalist collaborationist sentiment to his advantage in both. According to Robert Fisk's material, Hitler was more tactful in his approach to the Irish than Churchill – always spelling Irish titles and names correctly, always cunningly sensitive about the psychology of Irish nationalism. But then if there was one thing that Adolf Hitler understood it was the spirit of nationalism.

Robert Fisk makes few judgements, preferring always to offer the annotated facts (some chapters have more than 200 sources quoted), and it is as a work of detailed actuality that this book will stand; but he does offer the theory that Ireland's approach to the Second World War was alarmingly lacking in moral content. The fate of the Jews is hardly mentioned and, indeed, hardly figured at the time; even after the death camps were opened up, some Irish newspapers claimed that these were propaganda exercises, fakes that the English concocted using starving Indians for the photographs.

But then, it seems to me, when people are faced with matters of tribal or national survival, morality is seldom considered:

survival alone counts. And as the novelist Elizabeth Bowen saw with unusual perception, in its own way Eire's survival as a nation was defined by its neutrality, and the struggle to remain neutral was also a struggle for identity survival and for self-respect.

There is much more to besaid on the subject, more reflections, more conclusions to be drawn, and Fisk's boook will be invaluable for writers and historians who will wish to analyse further the consequences of Ireland's position during the war. It is possible that, in the end, neutrality was the most useful policy for the Irish in the south at the time, and that it served – in the narrow yet survivalist spirit – the country's best interest. But there is a price for everything and the price of neutrality includes the perpetuation of differences with Northern Ireland and a relationship with Britain in which there is little trust; yet more than that, it also includes the enduring knowledge which becomes more and more obvious, that Ireland has to carry the moral burden of having been, in the perspective of world events, wrong.

In Time of War: Ireland, Ulster and the Price of Neutrality 1939-45. Andre Deutsch, London.

Mary Kenny's review in The Spectator. 4 June 1983

Cultural Ireland in the emergency

On the rare occasions when I was asked about my position on the war in Iraq, I replied that I was agnostic. It is very difficult to assess the moral impact of a war while it is going on.

When I was researching the biography of William Joyce, Lord Haw-Haw, I encountered perhaps two dozen anti-war, peace – and appeasement – movements existing in Britain in the late 1930s. These ranged from frankly pro-Fascist organisations such as Joyce's own National Socialists to left-wing and feminist organisations supported by Quakers and the Women's Peace Pledge Union, not to mention varieties of communists opposed to all 'imperialist wars'.

We now know that going to war against the Third Reich was unquestionably the right thing to do, both morally and, as it turned out, strategically. Not a week goes by – and on the cable TV channels, not a day goes by – but another triumphant aspect of the narrative of this war is replayed on our television screens. It is taken for granted that we all agree that to fight against the Reich was the correct position.

But it wasn't taken for granted in 1938–39: by no means. As Clair Wills points out in her informative study of neutral Ireland, neutrality was the 'popular choice' all over Continental Europe – as well as in Ireland.

I do not make this point to draw a parallel between the Second World War and the Middle East today: parallels are odious, and usually mistaken. Many people were appeasers and pacifists in 1938–39 because they saw a parallel with the First World War, and the waste of life that had ensued from a too-zealous political engagement. But I do know that how we see events today will, inevitably, be different from the way they will be seen in fifty or sixty years' time, and that is the great divide between journalism and history. I have departed from the instant judgements of journalism and come to see the wisdom of waiting for history's narrative.

This book by Clair Wills (who is the issue of an Irish mother and an English father) is a rich compilation of knowledge and information about 'that neutral island' from 1939 to 1945, and as she says at the outset, there was no other democratic choice for De Valera and Eire, in 1939, than neutrality. The country was solidly behind the neutral stance, and for Ireland to join the Allies would have caused the most bloody civil war. Weren't the IRA – including the teenage author Brendan Behan – trying to bomb Coventry, fighting for a United Ireland, in September 1939? They would certainly have gone to war within Ireland itself if neutrality had not been the policy.

However, neutrality can contain many nuances, and if it meant a cold indifference for some British observers (and some Irish ones, who felt that the Allies should have been positively supported), to many in Ireland it meant something vaguer: something between defiant independence and covert support for the Allied cause. There was certainly, behind the political scenes, quiet co-operation with Britain: but, as Wills points out, that itself was based on *realpolitik*. De Valera understood well the logic of geography. Ireland was only neutral by the grace of her position, and thus by the sacrificial efforts of the Royal Air Force. Had she been on the eastern, rather than the western, flank of Britain, her neutrality would quickly have suffered the same fate as that of Belgium, the Netherlands and Denmark.

Anyone interested in the question of Irish wartime neutrality will find this a rewarding study, and wide-ranging in many respects, although the politics are as much in the foreground as the culture. To be sure, the author has researched the works of Irish writers during this period and these are important: she has looked at once-significant writers such as George Shiels and Frank Carney; she has included material about the theatre, employment, food, recipes, censorship (a well-documented area), and such valuable statistics as rising rates of venereal disease (always a sign of population movement). The adverts reproduced from The Bell, the literary magazine published between 1940 and 1954, also tell their own story.

But there are plenty more bites of this cherry of 'cultural history' to be had: my mother, who lived through that neutral 'Emergency' (as it was known) in Dublin, recalled riotous cocktail parties, art vernissages, society balls, lunch at the Royal Hibernian Hotel, drinks at the Shelbourne, dinner at Jammet's, musical parties, bridge parties, fine art auctions, shopping, gossip, reckless love affairs, and working-class Dubliners with more cash than ever before because their relations were earning great wages making munitions in Liverpool. The *Irish Tatler & Sketch* magazine is itself quite a resource for a picture of cultural and social life in Dublin.

For the mood of the time, Wills, like others before her, relies rather too much on the testimony of Elizabeth Bowen, the novelist, who was a British spy in Ireland at the time. Bowen wrote well, but she had scant feeling for grass-roots Ireland (indeed, she rather despised the mere Irishry) and was hostile to Catholicism, which still represented the majority faith and culture of ordinary people, even if hostility towards it may be routine for an intellectual.

That Neutral Island: A Cultural History of Ireland During the
Second World War
By Clair Wills. London 2007.

Published in the Literary Review, May 2007.

AN UNAMBIVALENT
JUDGEMENT ON DEV

The famous story of the Irish air crew in a dogfight over the Channel thanking God that De Valera had kept Ireland out of the war illustrates a significant Irish capacity for ambivalence: on the one hand, the majority of the Irish people were behind their leader, Eamon de Valera, in committing to neutrality during the Second World War. On the other, Irish people were – and remain – proud of the number of Irishmen who voluntarily joined the Allies, and showed bravery too: men from 'Eire' as the Republic of Ireland was then called, won seven V.C.s for outstanding courage; there was one VC awarded to a Northern Irishman, although the recipient (being a Catholic) was denied a ceremonial welcome by the Mayor of Belfast because he was a 'Taig'.

Brian Girvin, however, is not inclined to ambivalence in his trenchant new examination of that period, known in Ireland as "The Emergency". Earlier chroniclers of Irish neutrality, including Robert Fisk and Joseph Carroll, have been perhaps more forgiving of De Valera: Dev was autocratic, and unyielding in his defence of neutrality, but underneath it all, he gave some covert support to the Allies, and knew when to turn a judicious blind eye.

But Girvin's thesis is an unvarnished indictment of Eamon de Valera's stewardship of wartime Ireland The sum of his charge is that De Valera was a narrow-minded bigot whose fettered mentality could see no further than the dreary steeples of Fermanagh and Tyrone. And he was surrounded by even more narrow-minded bigots, notably his Defence Minister Frank Aiken, a mean-spirted stinker who scanned the deaths columns of Irish newspapers to make sure than none of the entries for those who died in the Emergency actually alluded to the war. Aiken, a product of those dreary Tyrone steeples, actually hoped the British would lose the war, and De Valera thought at one point that they would (as did not a few Englishmen).

The IRA actually declared war on Britain before the Lufwaffe, in January 1939, and actively supported Germany on the ground that 'the enemies of England are the friends of Ireland'. Dan Breen, an old gunman from the 1920s and much venerated by Irish republicans, wept the day that Adolf Hitler was pronounced dead. But De Valera did worse, in a way: he committed the public-relaitons faux pas of his life when he called at the German Legation in Dublin to express public condolences at the death of the Fuehrer, even as the concentration camps were being opened to the gaze of an appalled world.

If there are academies for spin-doctors, this episode should be taught in them as an example of how you can ruin an entire life's work with one ill-judged public gesture. Dev was not, privately, pro-Nazi; but he was a literal-minded mathematician, stubborn, self-willed, authoritarian and sometimes contrarious. He would not take advice from those civil servants who begged him not to do it: he insisted that it was "correct form"; even the Germans were embarrassed, in truth.

Girvin does not analyse this disastrous episode as others have done – as a dreadful gaffe and a misjudgement. He perceives it as characteristic of De Valera's lamentable impact on Ireland, from 1917 until he died in 1975, and perhaps beyond. The Hitler condolence was not, for this historian, an aberration, but a metaphor of the Dev regime.

Brian Girvin's book is meticulously researched and he has uncovered new material from a variety of archives. This is a period being examined by a new generation of Irish historians, who are less shackled by the nationalist ideology of former times. Girvin demonstrates how the policy of neutrality enabled De Valera's Fianna Fail party to tighten its grip on every aspect of Irish life. He also provides evidence that the British would have handed over Northern Ireland, lock, stock and barrel, if they could have budged Dev on neutrality.

There could be a more indulgent interpretation of Dev's ill-judged condolence gesture. Eduard Hempel, the German envoy, a career diplomat and his wife Eva were personally liked in Dublin. My mother thought it unkind that Dublin socialites, who had been happy to accept the Hempels' hospitality during the 'Emergency' afterwards crossed Grafton Street to avoid Eva Hempel. Mother mentioned this to the Archbishop of Dublin, and he replied: 'Then I shall call on her myself.' Dr McQuaid made a private visit to Frau Hempel, not to express condolence about the Fuehrer, but to say that all are entitled to Christian compassion. Dev could have quietly shown charitable feelings towards the Hempels, if he liked them personally. But that wasn't his way. He had to go and draw the world's attention to a most ambivalent chapter in Irish history, and the world took the worst possible view of it.

The Emergency: Neutral Ireland 1939-45. By Brian Girvin. Macmillan, London.

The Literary Review. May 2006.

Spies in Ireland

It was the late Lord Deedes who once succinctly explained to me what it was like to live through the Second World War. I had said to him "Those Battle of Britain boys were so brave..." And he had replied, almost impatiently, "No, it wasn't bravery we felt. It was a strange, deep, primitive compulsion that we were up against it. We had our backs to the wall. It was us or them."

To any defender of Irish neutrality during the Second World War – among whom I would count myself – the Deedes doctrine explains everything. It particularly illuminates Winston Churchill's leadership. He felt that compulsion – to defend the realm at all costs – in such a profound and magnified way that it enabled him to lead his imperilled nation with unique resolve. Churchill deplored Eire's neutrality, and remained enraged that Neville Chamberlain had restored the Atlantic ports to the Irish Free State in 1938, convinced that this was a danger to the security of the United Kingdom...

Inevitably, British intelligence spied on Ireland: Irish state intelligence was efficiently active too.

Eunan O'Halpin is the foremost living authority on intelligence networks in Ireland during the Second World War, and his book on the subject – dense and voluminous – is an invaluable souce of data for historians researching the subject and the period. Professor O'Halpin's knowledge is matchless, and we can be thankful that he has put his superb research at the service of historians.

Yet O'Halpin seems to know every inch of the wood without quite seeing the whole forest. He chronicles in great detail the spy networks – British and German – which criss-crossed Eire, particularly in the early phases of the war. Some of these characters were hilarious, such as Roddy Keith, an advertising man sent as SOE's 'whisperer' in Dublin, spreading rumours about Mussolini's insatiable sexual appetite for nurses; or Joseph Lenihan, the black sheep of a renowed Irish political family, a cheerfully anti-British British spy. Particularly entertaining were William Preetz and Joseph Donoghue, despatched by the Reich to Ireland, spending 'two dissolute weeks in Dublin blowing the Abwehr's money on women and drink': surely the best use of Nazi gold yet known.

There is a huge amount of incidental and often fascinating information: James Larkin, the idolised Irish Labour leader whose statue adorns O'Connell Street, was a Communist Party member, though Moscow found him somewhat 'unmanageable': as was the esteemed writer Peader O'Donnell. The Vatican did try to help individual Jews and there is some good Irish archival material on this. And Ireland's home intelligence network was often pretty effective.

But some of O'Halpin's own judgements are just personal opinions, sometimes perhaps prejudices. He dismisses Jimmy Thomas, the 1930s Dominions Secretary, as an 'erratic buffoon': I would say that Thomas – the illegitimate son of a domestic servant, raised by his impoverished grandmother, a washwoman, started work at the age of 9 and rose through his own efforts to become a Cabinet minister – was a decent politician who resigned on a point of honour, and was possessed of that unusual quality in public men: a sense of humour. O'Halpin describes the Marquis of Tavistock (of 1939) as a 'do-gooder': maybe so, but he was also a busy appeaser with some Fascist associations. He describes Guy Burgess as 'erratic but stimulating': yes, but a traitor just the same.

O'Halpin's main point of hostility is Winston Churchill, whom he sees at every turn as an enemy of Ireland. This, I would say, is unfair. Churchill championed Home Rule for Ireland from 1906 – he was hanged in effigy in Belfast for his views. He defended the Free State valiantly on the floor of the House of Commons in May 1922, as described in Mary Bromage's meticulous study of Churchill and Ireland. And later in the 1940s, Churchill spoke affectionately about the Irish state and praised its 'Roman Catholic civilisation'. The National Archives of Ireland also refer to Churchill's continued diplomatic support for Irish unity in 1948.

The big picture is that Churchill was entitled to do what he could to defend the United Kingdom in 1940-41: and the Irish Free State was entitled to choose its own terms for neutrality. Actually, 50,000 Irishmen volunteered to serve the Crown. An Irishman will often respond to a call of arms, but he's damned if he's going to be coerced.

Spying on Ireland by Eunan O'Halpin
Oxford University Press.

From MK's review in The Spectator. 28 June 2008.

OUR MAN IN BERLIN

Like all letters home, the mood in this very remarkable archive captures a moment when a dispatch is written, sometimes in all its guileless wrong-headedness, as when our man in Berlin, William Warnock, predicts repeatedly that England is finished. And him a Protestant and a Trinity College Dublin alumnus too! Behind the dry title of "Documents on Irish Foreign Policy" is some compelling narrative material composed of correspondence between Irish diplomats abroad and their political – and civil service – masters in Dublin.

The drama opens with tidings of war, and the declaration, by Taoiseach Eamon de Valera, that the 26 counties of Eire will stay neutral: in which he was endorsed by almost all of Dail Eireann and, evidently, by the nation at large. De Valera frequently indicates that he wishes to be benignly supportive of Britain, but he is particular in the way this benign supportiveness be expressed.

He will not, for example, allow the British "representative" in Ireland, Sir John Maffey (later Lord Rugby) to represent "the United Kingdom", for that would imply that Eire accepted Northern Ireland as part of the said "UK" entity. The grievous wound of Partition is Dev's obsession, and more than once, as Britain struggles alone against a mighty tyranny, it is subjected to lectures from the Irish about the injustice of a divided Ireland. Anthony Eden and Neville Chamberlain emerge from these pages as gentlemen of exquisite manners, always ready with an emollient phrase or a kindly personal letter to smooth ruffled Irish feathers.

It is no easy thing for a small country with weak defences to maintain its neutrality and Irish chippiness is understandable, if sometimes exasperating. Some Irish officials are easily vexed by taunting British press cartoons making fun of neutral Eire. The all-powerful mandarin at the Irish Department of External Affairs, Joseph Patrick Walshe, seems to be under the naïve illusion that London politicians can easily "curb" the press by diktat, perhaps because Eire found it an easy task to impose a draconian censorship on all publications. But if you are going to make a stand about a principle, you must accept the criticism that will inevitably go with it.

*   *   *

And so our diplomats abroad are given careful instructions about the presentation of (and motives for) Irish neutrality. Some reasons are practical and even politically wise: another Irish civil war might have ensued had Dublin joined the Allies. Neutrality signalled Ireland's long struggle for independence, and moreover, if Britain defends the rights of small nations, then Britain must respect the small nation nearest to her. Some reasons strike a modernist note: even before the 1948 UN declaration, the Irish had certain legal concepts of human rights.

But the self-exculpation is sometimes so finely wrought that one detects an element of discomfort, and certainly, the gradual realisation that neutrality can be a cold place when a civilisation is under siege. Pity our High Commissioner in Canada, John Joseph Hearne, who, facing pained expressions from the pro-British Mackenzie King – who holds that the war means a Christian civilisation against satanic paganism - is finally instructed by Walshe, to - "say nothing!...Keep off politics altogether."

In Washington, Robert Brennan (father of the writer Maeve Brennan) was subjected to increasing pro-British sentiment, even from some Irish-Americans. From Rome, London, Paris (and later Vichy), and Spain came Irish diplomatic reports, each a vivid snapshot of events as they unfolded: Sean Murphy's description of the evacuation of Paris is like a sideshow from *Suite Française*, and the level-headed Michael MacWhite reporting from Rome provides intelligent insights into Vatican politics and Italian paradoxes. The Irish legation is certain that the Holy Father (Pius XII) and the Vatican newspaper, *Osservatore Romano*, "support the Allies": and despite being at war against Britain, the Italians deplore I.R.A. terrorism in all its forms.

But from Berlin, William Warnock's dispatches are the most eye-popping. Because Ireland was still a Commonwealth Dominion, Irish envoys were not full Ambassadors, but Warnock had all the status of an Ambassador. He is correctly, even cordially, treated by the Reich. He is allowed his motor-car (a Ford V8) and 300 litres of petrol a month, although German roads by now had hardly any private vehicles.

Warnock, who died in 1986 after a successful diplomatic career, has an eye for everyday detail. He goes to cinema – where the German victories are all greeted by wild applause – shops at Christmas markets, notes the number of ladies' stockings allowed, reports on the conditions of railway workers, and is plentifully supplied with food. But although he is enough of a diplomat to cloak some of his political observations as disinterested – "it is said that", it is evident that he has gone badly native.

After the invasion of Poland, he writes that – "The man-in-the-street is profoundly and reverently thankful to [Adolf Hitler] for having brought Germany once more to a position of military greatness." Warnock seldom misses an opportunity to knock the Poles. "I understand from journalists of neutral countries that the Poles were guilty of indescribable barbarity in the German areas of West Prussen and Posen (the 'Corridor') before they retreated." Later he dwells on Polish lack of order and cleanliness in matters domestic, in contrast to the Germans. He suggests, in September 1939, that the war may be virtually over, and that, after Poland is crushed, "the British and French will retire gracefully, and will be glad to cut their losses." When Holland and Belgium are invaded he practically blames the Low Countries themselves and their Governments' "ill-concealed …enmity to Germany".

Warnock either swallowed German propaganda whole, or agreed with the Hitler project. He seems to accept casual caricatures about Jews. When Leslie Hore-Belisha leaves office in January 1940, Warnock reiterates the Nazi view of Hore-Belisha, who gave his name to the safe pedestrian crossing, as "a typical Jewish adventurer".

He suggests that German nationals in Southern Rhodesia are being held in custody because the governor, Sir Herbert Stanley, is "a Jew". He unblushingly recounts that Maud Gonne MacBride's autobiography is due for publication in Germany: but there are problems because the London publisher was a Jew.

Much of this is shocking now because we read with the reflective lens of hindsight: but these dispatches are revealing precisely because they are written in the spontaneously unguarded idiom of their time. Casual anti-Semitism was often accepted unthinkingly and in 1940, most people did believe that Britain would lose the war. The Irish DEA were convinced of Britain's coming defeat, and were making plans as to how they would proceed if – horrors! – a victorious Germany might even re-integrate Eire within the "United Kingdom".

While this work is published with scholarly intent, human stories and dramas abound. In Spain, envoy Leopold Kearney is absorbed by the task of visiting an imprisoned IRA man, Frank Ryan, who fought with the Republicans in the Spanish Civil War. Eventually, in an enigmatic move, Franco - who took a special interest in the case - has Ryan transported to Germany (where, after an abortive plan to land in Ireland in a German submarine, he died of TB in Dresden). Also in Madrid, financial succour is required from a destitute Irish citizen named Samuel Beckett – yes, it is he. A month later, in September 1940, the same Mr Beckett, now of 6, Rue des Favorites, Paris 15eme, asks the remaining Irish representative there, Count O'Kelly, to wire his brother in Dublin, requesting news – and an allowance of £20 a month.

Even more poignantly, there are pleas from a Mr James Joyce to the Geneva legation requesting assistance for his daughter, Lucia, to travel to England for psychiatric treatment. Before the Irish diplomats can proceed with any arrangements, James Joyce suddenly dies in January 1941.

Embedded with the serious political material (and matters of trade, security, communications, shipping) are many droll vignettes. In Washington, Brennan reports that Irving Berlin has produced a somewhat "mediocre" ditty called "God Bless America." In Ottawa, Hearne tells us that the Canadian people are pleased that Lord Tweedsmuir is to be succeeded as Governor-General by the Earl of Athlone. John Buchan had been ennobled by talent, but "Lord Athlone is the King's uncle", and it is so reassuring to have an aristocrat "of blood".

This work is a fine service to history, meticulously produced by highly regarded scholars; yet it also has something of the page-turner, leaving the reader cliff-hanging for the sequel. What will Warnock say when the tide turns against Germany (or, when the Irish legation is bombed to smithereens by "defeated" Britain in 1943)? How will the Irish in Vichy fare as the French Resistance gains momentum? How will the diplomats and mandarins react when the death camps are opened and the unspeakable cruelties revealed? Wait for Volume VII.

Documents on Irish Foreign Policy. Volume VI. 1939-1941. Editors: Catriona Crowe, Ronan Fanning, Michael Kennedy, Dermot Keogh, Eunan O'Halpin. Published by the Royal Irish Academy, Dublin.

Mary Kenny's review was published in the Times Literary Supplement, 26 June 2009.

Was Harry Patch right about war?

When Harry Patch, "the last Tommy of the trenches" died last week at the age of 111, he left a poignant heritage. In recent years he told whoever would listen that war was nothing but "organised murder" and that we should always resist going to war.

Many Christians – especially as the toll of death in Afghanistan mounts - would agree. I have just had a compelling letter from Eddie O'Hara in Bognor Regis who points out that Jesus Christ said we should love our enemies: war is indefensible for a true Christian.

Yes, and that was very much the prevailing mood during the 1930s. Contemporary values now disparage those who were "appeasers" during the 1930s, yet right up until 1940, all decent people were appeasers, including King George VI and Queen Elizabeth (very well documented in Andrew Roberts' *Eminent Churchillians*).

The French nation – in the overwhelming majority - were appeasers: like Harry Patch at 100, they rejected war. They had lost a million and a half men in the Great War, and the country was still black with widows' weeds and men horribly mutilated by the conflict. Marcel Déat – a socialist subsequently turned national-socialist – coined the phrase "Mourir pour Danzig?" ("Are we to die for Danzig?") when Poland was invaded, and the nation took up the slogan.

When Marshall Pétain decided that it was a lesser evil to co-operate with Germany than to fight it once more, again the majority of the French were wholeheartedly in agreement. Little children eagerly sang the welcoming anthem "Maréchal – nous voilà!"

But history marched on, and in the end, it became inevitable that someone would have to face Hitler's Reich in combat. A Just War? I think so: though no war is without its terrible cost.

All old soldiers say that war is appalling: they always have done. They are right. It is. All wars are ghastly. Many wars are morally wrong, too. But there may come a time when war is inevitable, and the natural law compels you to defend your very civilisation.

Choosing wrongly can put you on the wrong side of history. All those who embraced "peace" in the 1930s are now described as appeasers, covert Fascists, or stony-faced neutralists who allowed the Jews and the Slavs to be exterminated by an evil power. The French nation has often been condemned for surrendering in 1940. Pétain is now one of the villains of history. But that is what peace and appeasement can lead to: surrender.

Harry Patch's opinion was respected because he had lived through the hell that was Paschendale. Christians often admirably uphold the cause of peace. But never to go to war would mean that tyrants ruled the world, and I am not sure that is a very moral outcome either.

MK in The Catholic Herald.
31 July 2009